Knowledge Management and Organizational Learning

Volume 16

This series is introduced by the International Association for Knowledge Management (www.IAKM.net) with an aim to offer advanced peer-reviewed reference books to researchers, practitioners and students in the field of knowledge management in organizations. Both discussions of new theories and advances in the field, as well as reviews of the state-of-the art will be featured regularly. Particularly, the books will be open to these contributions: Reviews of the state-of-the art (i.e. syntheses of recent studies on a topic, classifications and discussions of theories, approaches and methods, etc.) that can both serve as a reference and allow opening new horizons Discussions on new theories and methods of scientific research in organisational knowledge management Critical reviews of empirical evidence and empirical validations of theories Contributions that build a bridge between the various disciplines and fields that converge towards knowledge management (i.e.: computer science, cognitive sciences, economics, other management fields, etc.) and propose the development of a common background of notions, concepts and scientific methods Surveys of new practical methods that can inspire practitioners and researchers in their applications of knowledge management methods in companies and public services.

This is a SCOPUS-indexed book series.

Marco Valeri

Organizations and Knowledge Management

Springer

Marco Valeri
Department of Politics, Law, Social Sciences and Humanities
Niccolò Cusano University
Rome, Italy

ISSN 2199-8663 ISSN 2199-8671 (electronic)
Knowledge Management and Organizational Learning
ISBN 978-3-031-97953-8 ISBN 978-3-031-97954-5 (eBook)
https://doi.org/10.1007/978-3-031-97954-5

This Springer imprint is published by the registered company Springer Nature Switzerland AG
The registered company address is: Gewerbestrasse 11, 6330 Cham, Switzerland

Foreword

The accelerated development of the knowledge economy demonstrated the dominance of knowledge and all the other intangible resources in the new industrial contexts created by information technologies and the shift from products to services. The evolutionary transition from industrial organizations to knowledge-intensive organizations imposed a definitive change from industrial management created by Taylor to knowledge management, whose pioneers were Peter Drucker, Michael Polanyi, Peter Senge, Chris Argyris, Dorothy Leonard-Barton, Ikujiro Nonaka, Hirotaka Takeuchi, Thomas Davenport, and Laurence Prusak. If Peter Drucker had the intuition of introducing the idea of the *knowledge economy*, and Michael Polanyi proposed the paradigm of the *tacit dimension*, Ikujiro Nonaka introduced the paradigm of *tacit knowledge-explicit knowledge* and developed the model for knowledge creation dynamics SECI (Socialization, Externalization, Combination, Internalization). The book of Ikujiro Nonaka and Hirotaka Takeuchi *The knowledge-creating company: How Japanese companies create the dynamics of innovation* (Oxford University Press, 1995) remains even today the fundamental work on knowledge management.

Industrial management focused on optimizing the use of tangible resources, which were rare and limited. Also, Taylor introduced from engineering deterministic thinking and from economics linear operations. Knowledge is an intangible resource, and it is not limited. Knowledge is a nonlinear field that exists through three basic forms: rational knowledge, emotional knowledge, and spiritual knowledge. This knowledge triad extends the well-known dyad created by Nonaka composed of tacit knowledge and explicit knowledge. Therefore, *knowledge management* emerged as a new research and practice domain capable of dealing with intangible, nonlinear, and unlimited organizational resources. A knowledge-intensive organization cannot be conceived as a machine anymore, as was the case with the industrial organization. It is an open system capable of generating and transferring knowledge toward society and of creating knowledge ecosystems.

A knowledge management system is composed of human and technological elements that are in a continuous interaction. The emergence of generative artificial intelligence (GenAI) challenged knowledge management systems with the generation of *artificial knowledge* and the need of its integration with human knowledge. Artificial knowledge is exclusively rational, and it is generated by algorithms based on syntactic rules. If human knowledge is considered generically a *justified true belief*, artificial knowledge does not reflect any truth. It can be wrong sometimes, even if it is correctly produced by the algorithm.

The main processes of any knowledge management system are the following: knowledge creation by people, or knowledge generation by computers and their algorithms, knowledge acquisition, knowledge storage and retrieval, knowledge sharing, knowledge transfer, knowledge translation, knowledge transformation, and knowledge use. Knowledge is a result of learning or unlearning. Knowledge creation is a complex process of experiential learning and then of transforming tacit knowledge into explicit knowledge using metaphorical thinking and natural or symbolic languages. Tacit knowledge is personal and embodied, and hard to transfer. Explicit knowledge is codified knowledge, and due to this property, it can be transferred between people. While knowledge transfer is a general process of knowledge distribution, knowledge sharing is a particular process where an individual is willing to share his experience with other people. Knowledge sharing is in competition with knowledge hiding and knowledge hoarding, as a result of the pressure put by competition and organizational culture on employees. Knowledge acquisition means to purchase knowledge from the external environment when the internal knowledge is not enough. That can be done through different forms, including hiring people with experience or exchanging knowledge within business networks. Knowledge transformation involves thermodynamics processes of converting one form of knowledge into another one, like transforming tacit knowledge into explicit knowledge, or transforming emotional knowledge into rational knowledge.

Knowledge dynamics reflects all types of knowledge transformations as well as knowledge variation in time and space, within organizations. In the well-known SECI model developed by Ikujiro Nonaka and further developed together with Hirotaka Takeuchi, tacit knowledge is transferred between people as a result of their social proximity. Then, tacit knowledge is transformed into explicit knowledge through externalization, at the individual level. Explicit knowledge is transferred from individuals within some social contexts and amplified through combination. Finally, explicit knowledge is transformed into tacit knowledge. In time, this cycle creates a knowledge spiral. Knowledge dynamics plays an important role in decision-making, especially through the reciprocal transformations of rational, emotional, and spiritual knowledge.

Knowledge use represents the final stage of any knowledge management system. Knowledge is embedded in products and services, and through them, in creating value for society. Knowledge-intensive organizations depart from industrial organizations both through their structure and their governance. Hierarchical and rigid structures have been replaced by horizontal and fluid ones, and knowledge governance has replaced deterministic industrial management. Knowledge strategies are the core of any business strategy, and knowledge leaders aim at integrating individuals' knowledge into efficient organizational knowledge structures.

Marco Valeri, a well-known international professor, and successful book editor, offers us a synthetic introduction to all the above processes and phenomena covered by the umbrella of knowledge management. Being aware of the importance of knowledge, knowledge dynamics, and knowledge management for the efficient governance of organizations, Marco Valeri discusses the evolution of organizations from the Taylorist type up to the learning organization described by Peter Senge. Knowledge management is the new capacity of dealing with intangible resources and creating value for society.

Competing Interests The author has no competing interests to declare that are relevant to the content of this manuscript.

UNESCO Department for Business Administration
Bucharest University of Economic Studies
Bucharest, Romania
University of Padova
Padova, Italy

Constantin Bratianu

Introduction

The essence of the evolution of an organization is constituted by the ability to learn, by the sedimentation of new knowledge useful for supporting new behaviors capable of guaranteeing success in the competitive context. The organization changes as it learns or continuously regenerates its knowledge in architectures of meaning that change, as a form of existence rather than as a reproduction of its evolutionary nature. In the current competitive context, the true evaluation of an organization is no longer based on the accounting of traditional assets, but rather the value of the organization is determined by the ability to translate information into new knowledge.

The competitive advantage is linked to the skills that an organization can express, not only allowing it to seize the opportunities that arise and to supply high-quality services and products, but also to create new opportunities, new services, and new products. The attention thus shifts to the company's ability to recognize the decisive importance of the human capital made up of people and their knowledge, and the strategic nature of exploiting their potential. The value that this capital can develop is decisive for organizational evolution, but it is equally alien to classical economic laws, in which the levers and references continue to be known, even if not therefore easily governable. The laws of development are not only equally complex but also provide intervention levers that act on different aspects of the organization: reward system, processes, organizational structure, and behavior models. And in any case, at the basis of everything, corporate identity reigns, the sharing of values. Everything that in the past could be considered accessory but useful now becomes necessary. A reward system that is inadequate in relation to company objectives, the market, and staff expectations both slows down and hinders the achievement of pre-established results and causes much worse damage as it leads to the immediate loss of precious cognitive capital, in some cases irreversibly.

Knowledge management process can be categorized into knowledge creation, knowledge validation, knowledge presentation, knowledge distribution, and knowledge application activities. To capitalize on knowledge, an organization must be swift in balancing its knowledge management activities.

Learning organization needs routines and procedures without which it would lose the direction of travel and the memory of the path taken, but it needs routines that are hypotheses to be tested, not administrative dogmas to be subjected to or circumvented. Routines are the seat, although not exclusive of the organizational memory of organizations. Routines are the product of the evolutionary process that each organization goes through. The organization can be read as an architecture of routines, each routine incorporates the knowledge that is produced daily. The system of routines, like knowledge, is dynamic. Every time a routine is activated and produces concrete effects, these are evaluated and based on the outcome of this evaluation, the effect will be either the maintenance of the routine in the repertoire or the replacement of said routine with another that incorporates new knowledge. Operational experience will show which working rules are the most suitable for carrying out certain operations and where instead an improvement effort is necessary aimed at achieving a dimension of greater adequacy to the competitive context.

One of the problems that organizations face today is understanding how to maintain the level of success achieved, that is, finding an organizational model that makes them capable of innovating to be dynamically successful. The old management models have become old iron and the hierarchical-functional structure no longer has any reason to exist: everything is fluid, changeable, and unpredictable.

How can the annual sales forecasting system, still used by many firms, support the change process of a knowledge-based organization?

Assets are no longer tangible but completely intangible. Today the knowledge revolution has changed the rules of competition. In the new reality the workforce is no longer made up of mere executors, but it is based on true knowledge operators. The modern managerial challenge, in fact, is based on the ability to draw new maps and, having thrown away the old tools, on knowing how to reinvent one's organization, one's business, oneself. From here emerges the need to ask new questions aimed at the future. It is important to be aware that in the age of knowledge, products will have an ever-increasing intelligence content. The product is intelligent because it is able, through the processing of a large amount of data, to offer structured information in such a way as to facilitate the consumer in its correct use, thus allowing him to derive maximum benefit. Products become interactive, that is, the more they are used, the more intelligent they become: this allows for the right customization. Furthermore, thanks to the use of intelligent products, the consumer will be able to facilitate their learning process. Customer needs are difficult to define and the distinction between what they want and what they really need is increasingly complex.

The book analyzes the evolution of organizations from the Taylorist type up to the learning organization described by Peter Senge considering all processes and phenomena covered by the umbrella of knowledge management to support the efficient governance of organizations.

The approach proposed in this book considers the organization as a circuit of circular relationships characterized by considerable interactivity toward and from the outside. The system that does not renew itself, which makes use of pre-established and pre-existing elements of the system itself, has a limited degree of freedom. On the contrary, a relatively autonomous, or evolutionary, system which tends toward emancipation has a much wider field of possibilities available to it as it can build the elements it needs. An organization is more likely to interact constructively with the environment the more diversified and differentiated its internal structure is. From this comes the learning process which involves the constant and continuous reproduction of those values, that knowledge, those mechanisms useful for dealing with the disorder that characterizes the competitive context.

The book is structured in five chapters.

The first chapter titled *Neo-modernism impact on organizational design* focuses on the key theories of organization collected in three primary phases: the modernist phase, which includes the classical school; the neoclassical school from the post-Ford era; and, lastly, the contemporary and interdisciplinary approach that incorporates theories related to knowledge management and learning organizations. The different strategies suggested can be viewed as efforts to address a fundamental and widespread issue that has consistently been a concern for all organizations. This issue revolves around selecting the organizational variables to target for intervention, aiming to facilitate structural change and enhance performance levels.

The second chapter titled *Complexity and Knowledge* analyzes how organizations encounter intricate challenges that impact their long-term survival. Complexed scenarios are marked by ambiguity and a deficiency of understanding and clarity. By expressing information and generating knowledge, organizations can tackle complexity, thereby enhancing their potential for sustainability. Information is expressed through organized approaches to inquiry, and within the field of systems, there has been considerable research into techniques that generate information.

The third chapter titled *Learning and Organizational Strategy* analyzes a framework for organizational learning that aids in the strategic management process. Organizational learning can be classified into two strategically important categories: external and internal. These categories encompass complementary processes. External learning emphasizes four strategically important areas of the organizational landscape: customers, competitors, networks, and institutions. Internal learning encompasses various types, including individual, intra-functional, inter-functional, and multilevel learning. Consequently, a key responsibility of strategic management is to guide the organizational learning process. This involves recognizing and distributing resources to essential areas of learning within the organization, which are vital for developing the capabilities required to attain a sustainable competitive edge.

The fourth chapter titled *Knowledge Governance* focuses on how knowledge governance, both formal and informal, affects knowledge sharing. Knowledge governance refers to a system within an organization that outlines both formally and informally how the company oversees activities associated with knowledge. As a result, it plays a crucial role in facilitating knowledge sharing. The creation and sharing of knowledge become the core of the company's functioning. They have in common the fact that they cannot be imposed, but they are realized only if voluntary forms of cooperation are guaranteed. The knowledge thus acquired can be used as a real resource by the company, which can reveal its potential only if properly managed and with a guarantee of its circulation.

The fifth chapter titled *AI and Knowledge Management in Modern Organizations* explores the impact of artificial intelligence on knowledge sharing to improve the organizational performance in modern organizations. Organizations can efficiently oversee physical resources by employing strategic tools to examine intricate tangible elements, including tacit knowledge. Nonetheless, there are obstacles in distributing resources for knowledge-related activities due to the challenge of measuring how concrete the results of knowledge exchanges are in relation to the units used for tangible resources. The recognition that the economy is transitioning from conventional markets to a cutting-edge knowledge-driven marketplace is compelling justification to adopt knowledge as a lasting strategy for maintaining market presence and competitive advantage.

Contents

Neo-Modernism Impact on Organizational Design

1

1.1 Organization Phenomenon

Organizational phenomenon is a key characteristic of contemporary, advanced, and industrialized societies. The organizational element has consistently been the focus of scientific investigation, with growing emphasis on the dynamic dimensions of business management studied through empirical observation. These analyses facilitate an understanding of how both public and private business administrations are defined not only by their formal, established structures that enable their operations but also by a natural inclination to adjust to local changes for the sake of self-preservation. This adaptability is crucial for ensuring that the business administration meets its objectives (Rainey et al., 1976; Andrews et al., 2011; Valeri, 2021).

The organization can be viewed as a system designed to generate responses based on all internal and external influences that affect it. The ongoing rapid pace of technological advancements, combined with the evolving nature of society, the environment, and the market, necessitates that today's management frameworks facilitate continuous learning. This approach is essential for effectively navigating various challenges and achieving satisfactory results.

The factors in the environment that can affect an organization can be categorized into two types: internal and external.

Internal environmental factors include the elements that, traditionally, form an organization: members, purposes, tools, and structure. These factors are different from the external ones because they are, above all, unlike the external environment, generally controlled directly by the organization. For example, by a particular outline of organizational culture, a leadership style, and a corporate *mission*, it could be possible to model several types of organizational systems: consequently, the internal environment will have an impact on the activities of the organization, its decision-making strategies, and ultimately the actions of both the organization and its members.

M. Valeri, *Organizations and Knowledge Management*, Knowledge Management and Organizational Learning 16, https://doi.org/10.1007/978-3-031-97954-5_1

External environmental factors refer to all circumstances outside of the organization that can nonetheless impact its operations.

These factors, in fact, although taking place outside the organization, can have a considerable influence on the organization development, on its functioning, and on the system *sustainability* in the long-term perspective. These elements are particularly associated with the economic environment, technological advancements, political and social surroundings, market influence, and competition.

Every organization eventually faces these pressures, and to ensure its continued existence, it must comprehend them and deliver appropriate and timely responses. If these external factors are overlooked or not sufficiently considered, it could lead to adverse effects on the organization. The essential element for guaranteeing the development, progression, and longevity of the system lies in embracing a proactive mindset. This mindset promotes adjustments and decision-making that seek to avert issues, favoring this approach over a reactive one that only addresses problems after they occur (Selznick, 1964).

The external factors that an organization has to take always into account are:

Technology and its advancements have been evolving consistently over the past few decades. Despite the organization not being able to regulate the pace and extent of these developments, it must enhance its capacity to stay informed about the most effective technologies available and leverage them optimally.

Political and social context: Any modifications, especially those of a political nature, can significantly affect an organization or a specific industry. In light of this, the organization must not only anticipate changes but also be structured to respond to them (which are often unforeseen) with agility.

Economic context: A struggling economy has led, for instance, to a decline in certain types of consumable products (such as recreational and leisure activities, luxury items, gifts, and real estate); although the organization cannot exert control over the economic landscape, it should aim to confront it by identifying potential risks and capitalizing on available opportunities while keeping as it is.

Clients and providers: They represent the most crucial components of the organization in terms of external operations. The suppliers significantly affect costs, and their influence on decision-making is contingent on the availability of requested resources and the level of demand. This, in turn, affects the potential for negotiation. On the other hand, customers are the group that can ultimately decide the organization's success, as they have the liberty to select between one organization and its rivals.

Competition: This can be viewed as one of the most significant dynamics in the marketplace since it has accompanied the organization from the beginning. While emerging businesses must be organized to effectively compete against more established and successful players in the industry, the latter must, in turn, be organized to thwart the advancement of these newcomers from overtaking them in a particular market segment.

By organizing the structure and operations of the organization, management can effectively influence the internal factors closely related to its function: the amount and quality of resources, employee motivation, staff productivity, and the selection of optimal or alternative objectives (Adinolfi, 2003). Regarding external factors, management cannot directly intervene. This means that managers must first have a comprehensive understanding of these factors' characteristics and then develop valid and practical alternatives to address potential external threats.

Concurrently, it will be crucial for them to communicate and inform the various project units about the factors that could affect its success, assigning them the responsibility of developing suitable action guidelines.

In any organization, both dynamic and static aspects exist together and constantly interact, ensuring smooth processes while simultaneously altering the very definition of what an organization is.

When describing it, it is essential to consider both perspectives. The two structures, dynamic and static, should be viewed as two facets of the same reality, as their connection is continuous and offers the potential for future contamination (Miles, 1975).

The structure only exists as far as it creates processes and objectives that to be achieved require a formalized and pre-established structure. Any organization, functioning as a social entity, is directed by its goals and structured around various projects and activities. Additionally, it engages with its external environment, which serves as another significant factor influencing the organization and its operations. In the upcoming chapters, it will be evident that shifts in the external and environmental context will drive significant advancements in thinking patterns and the implementation of organizational theories (Bourgeois, 1980; McAuley et al., 2017).

In recent decades, the organizational structure has undergone a modernization process driven by a trend of corporate and managerial reorganization. This shift has been essential due to the increasing complexity of the social environment, its ongoing transformations, and the emergence of new economic methods influenced by neoliberal ideals (Boulding, 1953; Stinchcombe, 1965; Brown & Eisenhardt, 1997).

Due to the ongoing development of organizational concepts and the continuous modernization of public administration, it can be asserted that, today, public administrations—specifically public organizations—are not entirely opposed to private organizations. Instead, they should be viewed as a representation of the category known as complex organizations (Etzioni, 1961).

The complex organization represents the evolution of the simple organization. To enhance and broaden its scope and capabilities, it incorporates complex elements through a process that enables the structuring of roles within formal frameworks aimed at this goal while simultaneously altering its objectives (Parsons, 1960).

Consequently, it is possible to analyze a transformation in organizational frameworks characterized by leadership and management roles, coupled with the growth of various organizational units; each is responsible for fulfilling one of the several objectives that the organization collectively aims to achieve (Anderson, 1999; Morelli, 2017).

The complex nature of the structure offers a further benefit to the organization, as this complexity enables it to more effectively handle uncertainty and disorder, viewing these factors as opportunities for enhancing adaptability and fostering innovation (Butera, 1977; Bonazzi, 1984; Robbins, 1990; Martinez, 2004; Martinez et al., 2017; Costa et al., 2016).

From this perspective, as previously stated, the relationship emerges between the formalization of organizational relationships (the static aspect) and the necessity for adaptable managerial structures, which enable responsiveness to change (the dynamic aspect) (Duncan, 1972; Sorenson et al., 2004; Siggelkow & Rivkin, 2005; Larsen et al., 2013).

In addition to this aspect, one can recognize the proximity between public and private organizations. The intricacy of an organization increases concurrently with the rise of its various levels, which interconnect and overlap based on vertical and horizontal growth and specialization pathways (Casalino, 2008; Aulich, 2011; Aguiari & Di Nauta, 2012; Rebora, 2017).

The evolution of organizational theories reflects a gradual move away from traditional pyramidal structures, which are rigidly hierarchical and follow a top-down power distribution. Instead, there is a shift toward horizontally developed organizational frameworks characterized by a flattening of the hierarchy. This transformation involves the removal of intermediate and subordinate decision-making and control levels, alongside the utilization of functional units that are granted increased autonomy.

The intricate structure of both public and private organizations can be defined by the following features: the organization's size, the existence of an administrative component, a confined and clearly defined scope of control, the specialization and standardization of tasks and procedures, centralization of decision-making power, structural differentiation, and formalization.

Particularly the final point seems indicative of the complexity within an organization. As complexity increases, there is a greater need to implement formal procedures and regulations to manage their dynamics (Daft et al., 2020). The requirement for formalization, which aligns with the organization's static aspects, must effectively engage with the demand for flexibility that embodies the dynamic components.

This adaptability is essential for the structure to adjust seamlessly to increasingly frequent changes while still maintaining. Regardless, when evaluating whether the notion of complex organization is applicable to public organizations, it is essential to recognize the significant differences in structure and behavior between public and private organizations (Cafferata, 1984, 1986; Butera & Dente, 2009; Mercurio & Martinez, 2009).

Public administration is especially responsible for a plurality of needs, having to consider in planning its actions of the existence of various interests, of the technical-organizational complexity as far as some public sectors are concerned, together with the fundamental equity principle, which should distinguish the decision-making process of any public organization (Bogason, 1998). Another key distinction is the asserted dominance of public administration, which does not interact with citizens on equal terms. While individuals are users of its services, they remain under its authority. Public administration acts thanks to the power ensued from a set of various regulatory rules, which impose the citizens equivalent commitment (Walker & Bozeman, 2011; Anderson, 2014).

While the shifts and dynamism in environmental, technological, social, and economic contexts have impacted the framework of public administration, it is important to acknowledge that it fundamentally relies on bureaucracy, as theorized by Max Weber, with remaining unchanged. Its structure is defined by objective and generic processes and rules, alongside predetermined roles that cannot be modified by the person presently in that role. The inherent rigidity of public administration and its adherence to the bureaucratic model have posed challenges, even with recent efforts to implement a managerial approach, particularly in the areas of planning and control (Aldrich, 1979). The transition has proven to be difficult.

From a planning standpoint, the absence of clearly defined and pre-planned objectives has rendered the management of the public structure ineffective and unproductive, leading to adverse impacts on various intermediate control levels that are not distinctly established or identifiable.

Another distinction between public and private administration emerges, particularly concerning the means and resources they need to acquire and utilize for their continued existence.

The impossibility to control the process during the different steps of its development, favoring only a check of the result, leads to the inconvenience of not being able to easily identify the *internal problems*, which makes the process more expensive (ineffective) or slower (inefficient).

1.2 Postmodernist Influences on Organizational Design

The evolution of the field of business organization has demonstrated that examining an organizational system is both an intriguing and challenging endeavor. Organizations are complex entities that cannot be attributed to just one interpretive framework. Beginning with the logical and scientific perspective put forth by the classical school, which draws on insights from fields like engineering, law, and economics, the organizational phenomenon and its theoretical underpinnings evolve. This development is further enhanced by the incorporation of more human-centered disciplines such as psychology and sociology while relying less on strictly scientific disciplines (Baldwin, 2012; Burton, 2013).

In this transformed environmental, cultural, and social landscape, the human relations school evolves alongside a field of study focused on examining the different aspects that shape organizational complexity. The goal is to better equip individuals to formulate suitable solutions to the challenges arising from the organization's operations, both in relation to its internal dynamics and its interactions with the surrounding environment (Miles, 1965, 1975; Miles & Snow, 1978).

It can be asserted that an organizational system is a structure marked by complexity and challenges, and thus only research grounded in scientific knowledge, utilizing an interdisciplinary theoretical framework, can provide a sufficient comprehension of this phenomenon.

Another objective resulting from the gradual abandonment of the traditional view is the idea that an organization's existence and operations are fundamentally shaped by its members. In essence, the organization consists of individuals who communicate with one another and their external environment, bound together by shared goals and objectives.

The shift away from classical perspectives is both a cause and a result of the emerging notion of the individual in the organization. This person transforms into a strategic asset and a proactive resource, ultimately proving to be more significant than financial capital and technological investments.

The development of the organizational theories underscores the persistent elements that appear in every line of thinking, particularly regarding the challenge of defining what organization truly means (Hecksher & Donnellon, 1994; Kanter, 1989; Clegg, 1990, Nohria & Berkley, 1994; Weick & Berlinger, 1989; Handy, 1989; Valeri, 2021).

The defining features of an organization are widely recognized and consist of a combination of human, financial, and technological resources. These elements interact in harmony with shared goals, organizing themselves through the allocation of roles and tasks directed toward achieving specific objectives. Based on these shared traits, the various theories will assign varying degrees of importance to the different elements of the organizational system, resulting in numerous structural models and recognizing a multitude of intervention variables.

The classical school, as discussed earlier, has introduced a perspective on organizational reality that is marked by a scientific and rational understanding of the phenomenon. The fundamental belief of the theorists from the classical school is that an organization consists of a structure, and its operations rely solely on this structure. Given that the structure is a component that can be intentionally and logically designed, it is both essential and adequate to make adjustments to the structure to align the organization's operations with the new market requirements.

According to the classical school, the purpose of the organization is to identify the organizational structure more consistent with the operational implementation of the corporate strategy, thus building a model (so-called one best way) universally applicable and replicable, since it is founded on a scientific and rational basis (Valeri, 2021).

The significant advantage of the evolution of organizational discipline is its recognition of the organization as a complex system. This necessitates a comprehensive reevaluation of strategy, considering not just the individual components in isolation but, more importantly, the interactions and mutual influences that arise among them.

These interactions are ultimately the foundation and core of the organizational system, retaining the number as it is. As has been stated multiple times, the traditional school of thought, particularly Taylorism, was primarily applied in the factories owned by industrialist Henry Ford. The concept of Fordism highlights the real-world application of Taylorism theory within large-scale industries, specifically in the automobile sector (Taylor, 1911). With Fordism, the concepts of scientific management introduced by Taylor were pushed to their limits, as it marked the emergence of a structured approach to industrial labor centered around the assembly line for the very first time.

The assembly line production method significantly decreased manufacturing times, which in turn led to reduced costs. Each component was systematically organized and set up in advance using scientific methods to ensure that the worker could avoid any extraneous movements.

In short, the worker had to be able to do *one thing with one movement*. Maximal emphasis is placed on the values of precision, respect, obedience, and total availability, which correspond to a relevant fragmentation, rationalization, and measurement of the working activity and performance. Each activity is divided and standardized, according to simple and well-defined times and methods, into *elementary* tasks that each individual is able to perform, in compliance with the typical Tayloristic *one best way* paradigm.

Theoretical insights from Taylor and practical applications from Ford led to the creation of an organizational framework that defined the entire progression of the second Industrial Revolution; however, this model quickly exposed its inherent drawbacks.

Critiques of the traditional model primarily highlight the significant alienation experienced by individuals, which stems from an organizational framework centered on the scientific division of labor. In the context of Taylorism, a person is viewed merely as a component of a machine, overlooking the unique aspects of human nature. As a result, Taylorism is increasingly viewed as a type of exploitation, where human capital is not appreciated for its full potential, leading to a decline in productivity for the organization.

People should no longer be viewed as mere cogs in the machine, as an organization thrives on their ambitions and actions, which are essential for its survival and functioning. The worker cannot therefore be reduced to the *homo oeconomicus* proposed by the classical school, whose only motivation is to maximize profits. The individual is a set of emotions, feelings, beliefs, and values that cannot be treated as all the other material resources of the organization are managed.

The traditional model encounters a crisis, creating space for organizational theories that advocate for viewing the organization as an open system, generally influenced by the principle of collaboration. The analysis now shifts its attention, at multiple levels, to the relational and interactive processes that shape the organizational framework, recognizing the significance of effectively and cohesively managing these elements to guarantee the organization's success.

The elements of organizational intervention are starting to broaden, encompassing not just the formal framework but also influencing the more genuine human elements within the organization. This applies to both the internal dynamics and the external interactions as well.

Organization needs to be seen as a system that is in ongoing interaction with its surrounding environment, which means it must implement organizational strategies that facilitate regular and continuous engagement with all its elements. Hierarchical framework suggested by the classical school starts to reveal its constraints when the surrounding environment becomes unpredictable, rather than stable, marked by significant instability and uncertainty.

This heightened level of uncertainty introduces an additional requirement for efficiency and effectiveness within the organization, aspects that were previously regarded as fundamental.

The updated benchmark emphasizes flexibility: a flexible framework is the only one capable of responding to changes in context without experiencing disruption, thereby using these circumstances as chances for innovation and growth (Mercurio, 2016).

In this context, the idea of cooperation is increasingly vital, paving the way for contemporary organizational theories that view knowledge and its flow as the true driving force behind an organization's productivity and longevity. The organization can only tackle the challenges of the new millennium by fostering relationships rooted in collaboration and shared goals, as relying solely on hierarchy and authority is insufficient for maintaining the cohesion vital to the organization's vitality and success (Sarti & Torre, 2018; Livijn, 2019; Berraies, 2020).

The rigid hierarchical and pyramidal organization demonstrates its shortcomings considering the transformed environmental, social, and economic landscape. This is because every action, piece of information, and interaction must navigate the entire hierarchy to enable leaders to connect with the grassroots level. This inevitably causes a decrease in the flow of information and knowledge, which ultimately hampers the overall productivity of the organization. Moreover, the significant divide between the different tiers, where subordination is intimately linked to the ideas of authority and control, along with highly formalized relationships, leads to the troubling outcome that individuals lack a clear understanding of their role in the production process; they only comprehend their specific and defined tasks.

The effectiveness of the cooperation model and the ongoing improvement of human resources, along with advancements in the social and technological landscape, result in a revitalization of the organizational frameworks utilized by businesses (Martini et al., 2017). These organizations increasingly aim to streamline their structures, promoting the establishment of staff roles that aid line positions, functioning as collaborative partners rather than subordinates.

Casual relationships gain significance, as they enable the direction of individuals' actions, encouraging them to work toward shared goals. In the earlier chapters, we discussed how business networks, franchising networks, and industrial districts are some of the most successful examples of organizational systems that are based on the principle of collaboration. These organizational facts clearly indicate that the traits of the modern economy and environment prevent the organization from viewing itself as a separate system, free from external influences.

The influences of the external environment are inescapable for the organization, necessitating management and governance just like any other important aspect of its operation. The modern world, characterized by globalization and the absence of national borders, alongside the swift and unyielding advancement of technology, has demonstrated that collaboration often emerges as the sole viable solution for ensuring survival in many instances.

1.3 Post-Industrialism and Post-Fordism: Genesis and Characteristics

The concepts of post-industrialism and post-Fordism typically pertain to the organizational changes that emerged following the collapse of the Fordist industrial model during the 1970s. These terms refer to a collection of cultural, social, and economic factors that, from the organization's perspective, emerge consistently, whether or not they are linked to previous events. The shift from Fordism to post-Fordism does not result in a distinct and abrupt separation; instead, it is driven by a viewpoint of growth and progression from historical practices to future possibilities.

In essence, we observe a comprehensive overhaul and update of the organizational elements that were found inadequate to tackle the difficulties arising from the altered social environment and the evolving market demands (Ouchi, 1981; Heydebrand, 1989).

The concepts of post-industrialism and post-Fordism represent distinct facets of the broader phenomenon of organizational evolution. This evolution can be traced from the classical school's proposed model to contemporary theories that view organizations as open systems anchored in cooperation. These theories typically align with the postmodern movement within the field of business organization.

Precisely, post-Fordism signals the conclusion of the large-scale industry organized according to the Fordist framework, examined from both an economic and production perspective. As factories steadily fade away, a hallmark of the traditional view of the Industrial Revolution, a novel economic model starts to emerge where most individuals are no longer solely engaged in the manufacturing of physical products. In addition to this production, the services market is growing, which, of course, cannot be structured according to the strict assembly line model established by Ford.

Post-industrialism signifies a shift in the degree of centralization and legitimacy of power, which is no longer limited to ownership or administrative frameworks. Instead, it increasingly transitions toward centers that possess knowledge. This is where the groundwork will be established to outline the concept of a learning organization, a contemporary organizational model that increasingly defines today's business structures. The concept of post-industrialism refers to the gradual reduction of the industrial model as it is traditionally perceived. This change results in the breakdown of class distinctions that emerged from industrial capitalism and massive factories.

The concepts of post-industrialism and post-Fordism are viewed as particular elements of the broader postmodern cultural movement, which is marked by an emphasis on the unpredictable facets of reality and a significant drive for transformation and innovation.

The emergence of postmodern culture serves as both a catalyst and a consequence of moving beyond the strict structure imposed by Fordism, leading to the embrace of flexible production systems that prioritize collaboration, adaptability to change, and a restructuring of hierarchical levels (Clegg, 1990; Meek, 2004; Crook et al., 1992; Hancock & Tyler, 2001).

Post-industrialism and post-Fordism represent the social and economic outcomes, respectively, of the growth of postmodernist culture, which has defined the organizational landscape since the latter half of the twentieth century. At this stage of industrial growth, there is a common recognition that the organizational framework based on the Fordist model cannot sufficiently address the global challenges arising from the vastness of the market, which in turn necessitates a shift and transformation in the organizational paradigm.

In a viewpoint that maintains continuity with conventional thought, there is an effort to modify production decisions to fit the altered environment, slowly moving away from the organizational framework rooted in the principles of scientific management and the inflexible production line.

The phase of industrial development known as post-Fordism is marked by the implementation of organizational standards and technologies that draw on the ideals of employee qualification, specialization, and adaptability.

This outcome stems from a gradual shift away from the Fordist viewpoint, which is marked by large-scale industrial manufacturing reliant on repetitive job functions. This approach had progressively diminished the qualifications and specialization of individual employees (Hecksher & Donnellon, 1994; Diefenbach & Sillince, 2011; Johnson et al., 2009).

Consequently, the company starts to gain increased flexibility in its organization and production processes, moving away from conventional mass production to better respond to a market demand that is becoming increasingly varied and experiencing swift changes. In an ever-evolving environment, the primary challenge is to guarantee the organization's swift reaction. Taylorism is gradually becoming less effective due to the increasing trends of large organizations relocating geographically and the decentralization of major factories into multiple organizational units, which are endowed with greater autonomy.

Post-Fordism and post-industrialism illustrate the innovative production phenomena we have observed during the shift toward the twenty-first century. This transition is marked by a significant degree of industrial automation and the adaptability of structures and organizational approaches. Additionally, there is a growing focus on the requirements of both consumers and employees, highlighting the importance of information, knowledge, and their dissemination (Marabelli et al., 2013; Gabel & Tokarski, 2014; Canonico et al., 2020).

Large business units *disintegrate* and decentralize into numerous smaller, increasingly independent subunits, while network organizational structures proliferate. Their stability ensures convenience for small, medium, and large enterprises alike, maintaining a supportive environment for operations.

As it has been emphasized repeatedly, the organization functions as a cooperative system that plays a crucial role in both interorganizational relationships—where direct and informal connections should take precedence—and intraorganizational relationships. In the latter context, individuals are not merely seen as subordinates bound by rigid rules; rather, they are regarded as active contributors who can offer valuable and innovative insights that extend beyond their designated responsibilities.

Nevertheless, it is essential to emphasize that the evolution of the postmodern view of business has not supplanted the Tayloristic approach, which, in fact, remains in use, albeit in various practical forms. This is true, for instance, in developing nations where the growth of organizational structures is still at an early stage. Post-Fordism and post-industrialism establish the groundwork for their evolution, drawing from historical and social origins, particularly the rapid advancement of information technologies characteristic of the twentieth century. This technological progress can be regarded as the primary and most significant catalyst for the transformations and innovations in social and productive structures.

The advancement and success of new technologies have essentially triggered a genuine revolution, drastically altering the entire environmental, social, and economic landscape. The slow and widespread growth of the Internet, along with its diverse range of applications, serves as a notable illustration. The ongoing expansion of the economic landscape and its associated variables have introduced novel challenges and complexities to post-Fordist structures, including a rising unemployment rate. This increase in joblessness is largely attributed to decreased labor demand, which has been influenced by the advent of new technologies (Canonico et al., 2012).

The adaptability of the organization, an increasingly essential aspect of its success, leads to a corresponding flexibility in production, which in turn results in a gradual instability of employment.

The dehumanization associated with Taylorism presents challenges for the post-Fordist organization as well, particularly concerning the impact of corporate decisions on its employees and society (Foss, 2003; Child, 2005). Organizational and management strategies are gaining traction with the goal of shortening the time to market, which refers to the duration from recognizing market demand to when the product or service becomes available. A production approach that truly represents the idea of flexibility is the inventory management system based on the so-called just-in-time model.

1.4 Post-Fordism Implications on Organizations

Post-Fordism and post-industrialism emerge as consequences of the increasing importance attributed to the individual within the organization. Rather than being viewed merely as a component of a machine, the individual is now seen as a valuable strategic asset that necessitates significant attention and investment.

This individualistic viewpoint serves to challenge conventional reference authorities, including those found within organizations, which are characterized by a hierarchical structure and a reliance on the principle of authority. An increase in independence, which is associated with heightened responsibility, is acknowledged for the individual employee.

Corporate organizations are starting to embrace organizational frameworks that favor a horizontal approach through employee groups, rather than the vertical and hierarchical structures that had characterized them until now (Clegg, 1990).

Furthermore, the human factor becomes more and more important, identifying the real engine of the organization's productivity. The worker's satisfaction and motivation are no longer considered merely *monetizable* in wage increases, but they understand how the individual needs continuous, effective, and constant stimuli and motivational support. This encourages the worker to feel part of the organization, asking him to actively contribute to its prosperity to achieve the common objectives.

The organization's governance and overall management should focus on achieving optimal levels of efficiency and effectiveness, but also they must direct their actions toward a progressive enhancement of human capital, investing in its training and in its stabilization, to ensure that all individuals move together aware that the behavior of one can influence that of the other and, in general, the whole organization (Valeri, 2021).

Moreover, the role of the human element is increasingly vital, as it plays a crucial part in determining the true driving force behind the organization's productivity. Employee satisfaction and motivation are now recognized as being more than just measurable through salary increases; it's understood that individuals require ongoing, efficient, and consistent encouragement and support to stay motivated. This motivates the employees to see themselves as members of the organization, urging them to engage actively in its success to reach shared goals.

The company's management and overall governance should focus not only on achieving optimal efficiency and effectiveness but also on the continuous improvement of human capital.

This involves investing in training and providing job stability to ensure that everyone works collaboratively, understanding that one person's actions can impact others and, ultimately, the organization as a whole (Vidal, 2007; Hancock & Tyler, 2001; Rickards & Clark, 2012).

From a management viewpoint, the ideas of coordination and cooperation are increasingly significant. Management is no longer limited to solely focusing, as in the Tayloristic approach, on implementing a scientific breakdown of tasks while exerting authority and control to adhere to set quantitative and time standards. From this new viewpoint, management should harness all the organization's energies and resources to reach shared objectives while also fostering employee motivation and satisfaction.

In this fresh viewpoint, the concept of leadership, viewed as a distinctly individual attribute capable of turning a manager into a leader, starts to emerge, somewhat opposing the idea of management. The leader is responsible for bringing together the different members of the organization, and this need for coordination grows as the complexity of the tasks assigned increases. Consequently, leadership should be capable of overseeing, assessing, and inspiring its employees to progressively enhance the organizational environment (Bonti & Cori, 2012).

Leadership can therefore be defined as the capacity to recognize the most suitable tasks for reaching goals while also considering their effect on employees.

Furthermore, the leader, to operate efficiently, must represent and convey the so-called vision of the organization, which allows workers to identify and perceive their role and contribution in the organization, with a natural virtuous boost to improve their skills and to take on greater and more relevant quantity of responsibility and autonomy.

Besides transmitting the so-called vision of the organization, the leader must prove to be also capable of transmitting the so-called mission: that is, the very reason of being of the organization, its most typical aims. By expressing the foundational mission of the organization, the leader can instill a sense of belonging and excitement among the team members. These emotional elements are just as significant in promoting the organization's success and sustainability (Elfenbein, 1998; Sy & Coté, 2004; Hakonsson et al., 2016).

The fundamental tasks of the leadership unit become *organization*, *planning*, *coordination*, and *control*. As post-Fordist and post-industrial frameworks evolve, leadership adopts new characteristics necessary for the efficient and effective management of organizations.

This transformation leverages insights from fields like psychology and sociology while also developing specialized skills in communication strategies to promote and guarantee a seamless integration between individuals and the organizational system, maintaining as it is. Discipline is no longer enforced through strict and authoritarian approaches characterized by passivity and subservience. Instead, it now operates through a subtle and ongoing influence that permeates all relationships and activities, aiming to foster a business environment conducive to innovation and transformation (Tagiuri & Litwin, 1968; Denison, 1996).

As the postmodern viewpoint evolves, an organization's fundamental value shifts toward its adaptability. This significant change in perspective leads to a transformation in management and leadership concepts, which are no longer solely designated, as in the Taylorist approach, to enforce discipline and adherence to work schedules and procedures. Indeed, it is increasingly essential for management to foster the creation of a unified and consistent organizational and productive atmosphere, driven by collaboration and alignment among different subunits.

These subunits should be guaranteed to operate independently while also functioning in a synergistic and interconnected manner.

Flexible Models of Production

The assurances of Taylorism and the accuracy of Max Weber's bureaucratic structure are starting to encounter challenges alongside the rising levels of risk and uncertainty associated with the ongoing expansion of the market.

These models are disrupted by the swift and ongoing advancements in technology, necessitating continuous revisions of work responsibilities and their associated materials (Bagguley, 1989; Crook et al., 1992). The outcome of this advancement is shown in the necessity for ongoing reorganization of organizational and work procedures. In this context, the division of the intricate system into multiple straightforward units, as suggested by the Tayloristic and bureaucratic approach, has proven to be insufficient.

In post-Fordist era, the swift advancement of technology leads, on the one hand, to the establishment of its dominance as a crucial and vital element, while, on the other hand, it enables the implementation of more adaptable and, consequently, more effective production methods. Additionally, the strategy for entering the market undergoes a significant transformation, shifting away from the traditional method of standardizing products and consumer demands. Instead, it focuses on producing goods in smaller quantities but with enhanced quality. Subsequently, sector-specific marketing is developed, targeting a particular market and consumer segment. This process necessitates a thorough understanding of the relevant sector, thus requiring effective information gathering and feedback mechanisms (Van Zandt, 1999; Kotler, 2000; Klahr & Kotovsky, 2013; Dobrajska et al., 2015).

Having a comprehensive understanding of the reference market also provides the benefit of being able to offer resources and stock products tailored to requirements, thereby reducing overall warehouse and structural expenses. In this altered environment, network organizational frameworks emerge, founded on the principles of collaboration, productive diversification, and decentralized decision-making.

With the decline of the Fordist model, significant adjustments to production processes are being implemented in organizations, largely driven by the emergence of new flexible forms of production. In Taylor's proposed model, production is attained through an organizational structure characterized by extensive fragmentation and a workforce with minimal skills. Tasks are broken down into straightforward and repetitive activities, significantly restricting the worker's autonomy.

Inside the organization, the separation between management and operational areas is established in a strict and distinct way, which governs its operations similarly to bureaucratic principles and relies on hierarchical control. It is also evident that there is a clear differentiation in the responsibilities of management, which is assigned to specialized managers. These individuals are responsible for integrating, overseeing, and coordinating the various complex production activities.

This organizational framework has demonstrated its highest effectiveness in large corporations focused on mass production. However, it has become evident that it falls short in the evolving economic environment, characterized by a decline in organization size, the demanding technological advancements that entail significant expenses for ongoing adaptation, and the increasingly expanding services market, which is no longer tied to the production of finished goods.

Since the 1970s, there has been a trend toward pluralization and diversification of production models due to the phenomena mentioned above. Therefore, one can refer to flexible specialization production models in contrast to the inflexible production model characterized by Fordism (Piore & Sabel, 1994; Kumar, 1995; Wood, 1989; Thompson & McHugh, 2009).

Flexible specialization is defined by the manufacturing of limited batches of customized products using machinery and equipment that can be adapted for various designs. Achieving flexible specialization indeed demands a workforce with highly developed skills. The traits of flexible specialization involve having multifunctional machinery along with a workforce that is both skilled and adaptable at the same time.

The effectiveness of this production approach primarily stems from the emergence of new electronic technologies that lower the expenses associated with implementing varied and flexible production methods. Utilizing this model, the implementation of multifunctional equipment and adaptable personnel results in decreased expenses in the manufacturing of customized and unique products targeted at specific market segments. This, in turn, promotes new investments in flexible technological solutions that can further lower costs and generate new market opportunities.

In flexible specialization, the primary challenge is to facilitate and encourage the ongoing integration of resources in a creative manner while maintaining a balance between competition and cooperation among different production units. In this altered environment, organizational frameworks like industrial districts emerge from the principle of decentralization (Atkinson, 1984; Kalleberg, 2003; Frenkel, 2003; Frenkel et al., 1998).

This organizational model is designed to meet the growing necessity for the organization to possess a flexible framework. This adaptability enables the organization to adjust to shifts in the external environment, particularly in response to the rapidly evolving market demands.

The expansion of decentralized networks or shared frameworks precisely addresses this requirement, as collaborating with rivals has proven to be a means of lowering costs and subsequently boosting the organization's productivity.

From this perspective, it is evident how these advancements are connected to the evolving notion of the organization, which is now viewed as an open system engaging with its external environment, fostering a continuous and mutual influence and interaction.

Flexible specialization emerges not only as an alternative theoretical framework for examining industrial transformation but also as a particular model of production organization that varies in form based on the context of institutional and productive operations.

This indicates that the method suggested by this model, which is based on a dynamic interplay between consumption and production, does not regard market structures as fixed elements that dictate a singular optimal strategy (one best way). In contrast, the flexible specialization viewpoint sees the market as a variable factor, shaped by the operational and competitive strategies employed by its participants.

In short, the adoption of flexible forms of production, in the sense analyzed so far, is accompanied by the tendency to a *fragmentation* of the mass market, to create a differentiated demand that can be satisfied through the constant introduction of innovative and high-quality products (Pollert, 1988, 1991; Thompson & McHugh, 2009; Gorz, 1999; Skorstad, 2009a, 2009b).

In an ever-evolving environment, where consumer demand fluctuates swiftly, investing in highly specialized equipment carries significant risks due to the heightened potential for product obsolescence.

The restructuring of the production industry is driven by an experimental mindset that results in the creation of innovative products and the capacity to swiftly adjust them in response to changes in market demand. Thus, it is essential to minimize the gap and, as a result, the interval between planning and execution.

This separation was distinctly defined and inflexible in the Fordist model, leading to a complex, rigid, and sluggish process for producing new goods.

New types of authority decentralization are being tested, leading to the establishment of numerous support units alongside a simplified central framework that is tasked solely with making strategic decisions. Organizational frameworks evolve around employee roles in a way that backs line positions and increasingly diverge from traditional pyramidal and hierarchical models, leaning more toward decentralized forms.

These modifications in structure and organization clearly entail an alteration in the internal arrangement of work. Production has shifted away from mass-scale operations characterized by uniform products and processes that can be divided into simple, repetitive tasks and responsibilities.

In contrast, production now focuses on highly specialized products made in limited quantities, necessitating continuous modifications to align with shifts in market demand.

In the present production landscape, the main priority is to reduce excess resources that contribute to rising costs across different areas without delivering adequate performance for the organization. To ensure this boost for innovation, it is necessary to reduce rejects, stocks, and waste, *lato sensu* (broadly considered), and to do so it is necessary to guarantee a strong degree of engagement and cooperation among the employees.

The worker has evolved from being the underqualified and undereducated individual essential for the operation of the Fordist organization. In the context of flexible specialization, the worker now demands a significant level of expertise and qualifications, along with a robust willingness to collaborate and adapt to various responsibilities.

In summary, the employee should be capable of handling various responsibilities, demonstrating flexibility to adjust to the organization's internal dynamics, including, for instance, the formation and dissolution of work teams based on production requirements.

Policies and protocols are put in place to encourage a collaborative attitude among staff, creating a positive and productive work environment while also improving individual learning skills. As flexible specialization evolves, organizations transform into genuine learning systems, shaped by a mix of formal and informal connections that boost the overall structure's ability to innovate.

The necessity for quick adaptation to abrupt shifts in market demand essentially calls for organizational transformation, which in turn requires skilled and knowledgeable personnel who can generate and disseminate information effectively.

The gradual focus on the knowledge theme is the premise on which the modern theory of *knowledge management* and *learning organization* is based, both based on the common belief that the creation of knowledge and its fluid circulation are the real determining factors for the success of an organization in the contemporary globalized context (Valeri, 2024; Rožman & Štrukelj, 2024).

1.5 Organizational Design and Decision-Making Process

The management of an organization consists of individuals who have management duties within the organization. They are responsible for overseeing the internal operations of the organization as well as the various factors in the surrounding environment.

As previously stated, a manager needs to demonstrate not just technical and professional skills but also personal attributes. These qualities include the capacity for reflection, interaction, and understanding, which enable them to engage more effectively with the organization's human resources. This approach promotes the integration of the various strengths of their colleagues and staff (Jones, 2013).

Alongside these traits, a crucial factor is the manager's strong strategic capabilities, which involve the ability to recognize opportunities within the organization and to take advantage of them effectively and adaptively.

This activity is solidified through the selection of a managerial strategy, specifically the decision regarding long-term goals that align with the organization's mission, which originates from a thorough understanding of the competitive landscape and a diligent assessment of the resources at hand (Hedelin & Allwood, 2002).

Thus, the manager needs to have effective planning and leadership abilities, be fully aware of the organization's mission, and show a strong inclination toward management and teamwork. Furthermore, he must possess significant creative capabilities that enable him to swiftly grasp the context and pinpoint appropriate solutions to the arising issues it generates (Citroen, 2011).

The management, consequently, defines the business goals and commits to their attainment, facilitating efficient coordination and ongoing oversight of the company's resources as well as the economic and social context (Shepherd & Rudd, 2014).

In the company context, this fundamental framework is reinforced by various initiatives aimed at achieving a balance between the resources at hand and the anticipated outcomes, thereby ensuring alignment with the organization's operations.

Management will consequently need to address additional essential processes, including the development of business strategy, budget planning, oversight of the activity report, and decisions regarding resource allocation. In each of these processes, it is essential for the manager to guarantee not only effective management of human resources but also a robust communication system with stakeholders, achieved through an ongoing and consistent development of the organizational infrastructure (Mintzberg et al., 1976).

As suggested by Fayol, the fundamental functions associated with management skills are *planning, organization, command, coordination,* and *control.*

Planning is the core of the manager's activity, consisting in determining the objectives and contents of the organization's operations carried out considering the possible and probable evolutions of the external environment and defining the consequent plans of action. The traits that ensure the effectiveness of these action plans include accuracy, alignment with overall goals, sustained effort over time, and the ability to adapt (Brozovic, 2018; Zhou & Wu, 2010).

Regardless of the situation, all managerial actions are executed via decision-making processes that involve recognizing and articulating the issues and requirements the organization needs to confront and fulfill (Eisenhardt & Zbaracki, 1992; Elbanna, 2006). The management's decision-making process should be organized using specific techniques that enable the selection of the most rational and ultimately optimal solution (Cohen et al., 1972).

Consequently, it is essential to recognize appropriate methods to investigate and address business challenges. Every decision-making process is segmented into three stages. The initial stage, known as *problem finding*, refers to the skill of recognizing and pinpointing the issue. In this initial stage, it is essential to pinpoint the different issues at hand and determine which of them should be prioritized for resolution. The problem identification stage is thus segmented into additional substages: pinpointing all instances that hinder the improvement process, systematically gathering data regarding these instances, and ultimately selecting the issue that requires the most urgent intervention. The second phase, often referred to as *problem setting*, involves the actual definition of the problem.

After pinpointing the situation to address through problem identification, this second phase involves analyzing the scenario along with the so-called trends, which refer to the underlying tendencies of specific behaviors. This analysis enables the identification of key areas and, as a result, facilitates the ongoing gathering of data that helps to accurately delineate the parameters of the issue at hand (Baligh & Burton, 1982; Holmstrom & Roberts, 1998; Robinson, 2008).

Once the issue is pinpointed (first phase) and is clearly defined (second phase), it is possible to enter the most sensitive and significant stage of the decision-making process, which is the problem-solving phase. The process of problem-solving involves a method of analysis designed to recognize, strategize, and execute the steps needed to reach a solution for the issue at hand.

The resources essential for effective problem-solving are twofold: in addition to measurement tools, which are used to analyze and gather information about the issue, there are intervention tools that aid in identifying and selecting potential solutions (Liedtka et al., 2013).

The initial step involves examining the present situation to recognize and specify the discrepancies from the optimal model, enabling the identification of potential causes. To perform this analysis, it is essential to gather information meticulously, serving as an effective tool in the following verification stage.

After gathering the available information, it is essential to conduct a diagnostic process to pinpoint the potential causes of the issue, identifying the most likely ones. Once the likely causes of the issue have been pinpointed, it becomes essential to seek potential solutions, particularly those where any action can yield the greatest benefits with the least resource expenditure.

At this stage, after pinpointing the issue, collecting relevant information, determining likely causes, and exploring potential solutions, it is essential to confront the key moment of this phase: selecting the most suitable solution to implement. During this stage, numerous methods are employed, including brainstorming, creation of diagrams, and collaborative teamwork.

In any case, the fundamental purpose of all these different schemes is to stimulate the recognition of multiple solutions, with an increasing level of creativity that allows to unhinge the problem and look for effective ways to deal with it, even by breaking away from the *rigid* schemes of the more classic and traditional solutions.

All these approaches rely on collaborative efforts, stemming from the idea that everyone has a constrained perspective on the issue at hand. By merging these viewpoints, it becomes feasible to attain a comprehensive and thorough understanding that considers all facets.

To ensure the effectiveness of these approaches, it is essential that the group, regardless of its organizational model, is properly managed and coordinated. This will help guarantee that efforts are focused solely on generating positive and constructive outcomes while avoiding conflicts or unresolvable extremes that are impractical.

This is another area where the manager focuses their efforts, encompassing both the direct supervision and training of work teams and the selection of collaborators and support roles involved in the specific resolution processes. This analytical process and identification of potential solutions result in a gradual refinement of options, involving a systematic elimination of those that are deemed less suitable.

During this selection process, the most effective solutions from those proposed will be recognized. After determining the optimal solution, it is essential to undergo a planning and development phase that reflects its actual operation. This involves pinpointing specific corrective measures to be executed, along with the timelines and methods for implementation.

In a contemporary organization that faces both fluctuating and ongoing external demands, this phase can be executed effectively—as previously noted—only if it is underpinned by a framework and composition that prioritize collaboration and adaptability. Once the selected solution has been strategized and implemented into the operational framework, it is essential to assess the outcomes and examine the legitimacy of the previously mentioned solution in this context. The stage of verifying and overseeing the outcomes is crucial, and for successful execution, it is essential that the information gathered, along with that obtained in the earlier stage, is thorough, meticulous, and unbiased (Grandori, 1999).

If the verification phase yields favorable outcomes concerning the anticipated results, it will be essential to persist with that course of action, standardizing it and potentially recognizing it as a model that can be utilized in other areas as well. Any standardization of crucial actions must always be accompanied by ongoing monitoring to ensure both their proper implementation and their continual alignment with the anticipated outcomes.

Herbert Simon (1947), in the elaboration of his theories on the organization based on the concept of the same as a system for processing information, aims at building a scientific theory of problem-solving and, in general, of the decision-making process, based on the belief that the human capacity for knowledge is constitutionally and naturally limited (Valeri, 2021). For this reason, Simon proposes the simplification of complex problems and the specialization of company structures, as the best activities.

1.6 Designing for Decision-Making

To manage the decision-making process, it is essential to pinpoint appropriate and efficient influence strategies that will help mitigate the inherent and natural constraints of rationality (Simon, 1960, 1967). One of the initial tools accessible to the organization is the division of labor, which addresses a universal principle of streamlining intricate processes and challenges.

By implementing the division of labor, fundamental to any organization, it becomes feasible to lower the level of knowledge and skills needed, allowing for a more precise alignment with the abilities possessed by individuals (Polanyi, 1966).

Indeed, the choice regarding the methods for dividing and structuring work is not merely a technical issue; it is a decision that carries significant practical implications, particularly in relation to the necessity of managing and coordinating the activities and outcomes of the entire organization (Bohanec et al., 2017).

For the division of labor to be efficient, organizational planning needs to be organized through the development of standardized procedures and actions that can steer the execution of individual tasks.

The efficacy of these procedures should be continuously evaluated, primarily relying on the expertise and specialization of the individuals involved in their standardization.

The extensive division of labor and the presence of established processes necessitate that management, while no longer bound by traditional notions of hierarchy, must still wield its own authority. This authority is perceived by employees as an acknowledgment of their willingness to have their actions shaped by the decisions of others. We refer to authority specifically because this level of acceptance needs to overlook the judgments and the extent of individuals' involvement concerning the decision that is to be executed.

Moreover, the degree of acceptance is what ultimately influences the success of an order or decision: the greater this inclination, the more attainable the operational outcomes.

To achieve a high degree of acceptance, the organization must implement appropriate incentives beyond just financial rewards. These incentives should encourage individuals to feel like integral members of a *system* that thrives and advances through the contributions of all.

While the idea of authority is essential, Simon recognizes the significance of various informal relationships that inherently develop within an organization, which help to support and integrate the formal structure.

Building on the contingent theories and the human relations approach (Valeri, 2021), the author emphasizes the significance of informal relationships. These connections do not arise from traditional notions of authority; instead, they are founded on elements such as solidarity, persuasion, and a shared sense of purpose and needs.

These social mechanisms serve as instruments for management, enabling them to inspire and motivate employees by convincing them that the overall growth of the organization guarantees the success of each individual member. The objective of fostering a sense of collective purpose and sharing can be accomplished by establishing an effective information system, supplemented by a continuous and thorough training and education program.

The development of precise information systems helps establish a competitive edge for the company by fostering a thorough understanding of its internal dynamics as well as the external landscape. This enables the company to anticipate and recognize potential changes, allowing it to address them with a mindset geared toward transformation and adaptability (Berman & Marshall, 2014).

An effective information system generally helps to lessen the bounds of rationality by ensuring a shared knowledge foundation for all members of the organization. This is achieved through the careful selection of essential and pertinent information flow that supports the decision-making process (Antonelli et al., 2018). Once a robust system has been established to form this shared foundation of knowledge, it is essential that this level of understanding does not become static as a completed achievement. Instead, there should be a continuous effort to refresh and enhance it, keeping in mind the goals of innovation and adaptation.

Consequently, in contemporary organizations, the establishment of training and learning systems is increasingly essential, as these serve as internal tools of influence for the organization. Through the development of these training programs, it is indeed feasible to enhance employees' feelings of belonging to the organization, highlighting the significance of each individual's contribution to its advancement.

Gaining knowledge is now more than merely a requirement for joining the organization and performing a role effectively; it has transformed into a true catalyst for change. Individuals no longer execute tasks in a routine manner; instead, they grasp the significance of their contributions within the larger framework, resulting in heightened motivation for ongoing improvement (Hull & Covin, 2010).

The development of effective learning systems enhances the flow of knowledge within and beyond the organization, encouraging its members to pursue ongoing improvement and increasing their capacity to assess situations and adapt to change (March, 1991).

In Simon's perspective, learning processes function in two distinct yet complementary manners: firstly, they enhance the knowledge of the organization's members; secondly, they incorporate new individuals whose arrival introduces knowledge that the organization lacked before.

The generation of knowledge is becoming increasingly significant in today's business organizations, as the world is in a constant state of flux. It is now more crucial than ever for organizations to maintain flexibility and quickly adapt to changes.

An in-depth understanding of the reference context is essential for anticipating potential changes and requests, allowing us to take proactive measures rather than simply reacting to them. In a general sense, knowledge serves as the essential foundation for the decision-making process, which, based on Simon's perspective, is truly the driving force behind organizational development.

In the traditional and logical view of organizations, decision-making is primarily held by the company's board and upper management, distinctly separated from the operational framework. However, when the company is viewed as an open system that emphasizes collaboration and adaptability, there is a shift in how decisions are made within the organizational framework. This structure is no longer rigidly hierarchical but rather more distributed, thanks to the creation of staff roles and overall support mechanisms, which are removed from conventional hierarchical structures (Etzioni, 1999; Calabrese et al., 2018).

Additionally, human capital is increasingly gaining significance, with individuals being granted higher levels of responsibility and autonomy. This shift ensures the establishment of a central framework that can focus primarily on analyzing strategic decisions and determining overarching guidelines.

The single members of the organization, thanks to the greater responsibility and autonomy recognized to them, increase their skills and their specialization, which also continues to be guaranteed not only through the division of labor, now less "scientific," but also thanks to an efficient learning and training system. As underlined by the theories of motivation, the organization's members receive further stimuli besides monetary incentive, and therefore they are more and more motivated and encouraged to a continuous and constant improvement.

This is a process of slowly distributing authority and decision-making power, leaning toward the establishment of more horizontal structures that evolve based on a vision driven by collaboration rather than hierarchy and control.

The motivations behind this process are primarily influenced by the progressive rise in the intricacy of the surroundings, along with a reference context that is becoming increasingly competitive, social, and economic, marked by a growing sense of instability and unpredictability (Hartmut, 2013).

The rising degree of instability and unpredictability has increasingly revealed the limitations of fixed frameworks like those suggested by models of scientific work organization. This underscores the importance of not just maintaining stability but also ensuring the flexibility of a business, keeping as it is.

1.7 Knowledge Generation in Organizations

Effectively managing the knowledge and teams within an enterprise poses both opportunities and challenges for today's businesses (Rofiaty, 2019). In the field of knowledge management, the obstacles vary from establishing and maintaining a knowledge management framework to the efficient use of tools and systems, as well as adapting to the organizational culture (Anjaria, 2020). In the context of an organization's teams and work groups, the obstacles encompass effective team leadership, creating and executing a collective vision and objectives, discovering methods to optimize productivity, and handling conflicts (Berraies & Chouiref, 2022). Every team member possesses a unique cognitive approach that influences how they evaluate circumstances, interpret information, and analyze results (Yao et al., 2021). They also bring varied viewpoints shaped by their educational backgrounds, experiences, areas of expertise, and personal values (Zhang & Wang, 2021). The essential factor in leveraging team diversity to promote innovation lies in exchanging the knowledge, viewpoints, skills, and insights of each team member. Ongoing knowledge exchange as a process facilitates reciprocal learning among team members (Min et al., 2021; Rožman & Štrukelj, 2024).

Teams that encourage knowledge sharing both within the organization and beyond often generate fresh ideas and enable initiatives that foster innovation. Innovative concepts must be transformed into concrete enhancements in processes, deliverables, and products (Jiang et al., 2016). Groups must determine which concepts to put into action and the methods to employ (Boamah et al., 2022). Teams with varied backgrounds possess greater knowledge and broader viewpoints, which facilitates well-informed decision-making and fosters constructive criticism. The group can subsequently reach an agreement on the implementation of new products, services, and practices (Zhang et al., 2020).

Teams that collectively believe in the importance of promoting change and creativity are more inclined to share innovative ideas, particularly when they receive backing from both team leadership and the organization's practices (Imam & Zaheer, 2021). Fostering psychological safety within the team enhances the confidence of each member and refines internal team dynamics related to knowledge sharing (Balde et al., 2018).

Teams that prioritize excellence as a fundamental principle and motivate their members to work together on execution tend to be more effective in bringing new ideas to fruition. Certain aspects of a team's environment, specifically trust, cohesion (Imam & Zaheer, 2021; Zhao & Detlor, 2021), and innovativeness (Min et al., 2021), have been recognized as factors that promote constructive behaviors among team members, including knowledge sharing (Xue et al., 2011).

Team members who perceive their colleagues as trustworthy are more inclined to develop strong social connections and demonstrate positive attitudes and behaviors during their interactions.

Relationships built on trust promote collaboration and dedication among team members (Balde et al., 2018). A trusting environment is crucial at the team level due to the significant amount of interdependence needed to accomplish shared team objectives (Koohang et al., 2017). Team cohesion denotes the sense of belonging, connection, integration, and mutual reliance that team members experience toward their group.

It creates a dynamic that influences the proximity of teammates, resulting in collaborative interactions and behaviors while minimizing conflicts (Xuc et al., 2011). Team innovativeness pertains to the extent to which team members are supported in proposing novel and enhanced methods of operation and are recognized for their contributions within the team (Berraies & Chouiref, 2022).

As organizations regularly adapt to evolving circumstances and teams take on the central role of navigating this transformation, fostering a climate of innovation within teams—marked by an openness to failure, a willingness to take risks, and the unhindered exchange of information—becomes essential.

Enterprises function in a knowledge-driven age where their ability to remain competitive hinges on how well they manage knowledge (Fischer et al., 2021; Henttonen et al., 2016; Muhammed & Zaim, 2020; Yin et al., 2020). Organizations need to foster a positive work environment that encourages employees to share their knowledge (Sahibzada et al., 2020). Additionally, organizations require employees who are committed, enthusiastic, and fully immersed in their tasks (Kim & Park, 2017), since involvement in knowledge management initiatives is considered a discretionary behavior and relies on the voluntary actions of the workforce (Xue et al., 2011).

Employee work engagement is recognized as a psychological state that demonstrates their willingness to invest effort in fulfilling their duties and working together with co-workers (Fait et al., 2021). Numerous research efforts have validated the role of work engagement on an individual basis in facilitating knowledge creation, sharing, and utilization at both personal and organizational levels (Acharya & Jena, 2016; Atapattu & Huybers, 2021). Contemporary businesses prioritize high-quality customer service and ongoing enhancements to their products, which help bridge the gap between knowledge workers and customers (Fischer et al., 2021). Effective communication abilities allow knowledge workers to collaborate closely with their colleagues during decision-making, goal-setting, and brainstorming activities (Al-Ghazali, 2020). The need for skilled workers to fill specialized positions creates both challenges and opportunities.

A significant challenge involves the recruitment and retention of knowledgeable staff (Amiri et al., 2020). As a significant shortage of skilled workers approaches, employers are compelled to seek more efficient methods for recruiting top talent and ensuring their long-term retention (Wei & Miraglia, 2017). Knowledge workers are crucial to the success of any organization. The unique expertise and understanding they possess are highly beneficial, as knowledge workers frequently lead the way in fostering innovation within the workplace (Nezafati et al., 2023). Employees with expertise will be the most significant assets for a twenty-first-century organization, due to their exceptional productivity, unique perspectives, and innovative thinking (Rožman & Štrukelj, 2024).

References

Acharya, A., & Jena, L. K. (2016). Employee engagement as an enabler of knowledge retention: Resource-based view towards organisational sustainability. *International Journal of Knowledge Management Studies, 7*(3/4), 238–256.

Adinolfi, P. (2003). Total quality management in public health care: A study of Italian and Irish hospitals. *Total Quality Management & Business Excellence, 14*(2), 141–150. https://doi.org/10.1080/1478336032000051322

Aguiari, R., & Di Nauta, P. (2012). Governing business dynamics in complex contexts. *Mercati e Competitività*, 1, Franco Angeli, Milano.

Al-Ghazali, B. M. (2020). Transformational leadership, career adaptability, job embeddedness and perceived career success: A serial mediation model. *Leadership & Organization Development Journal, 41*(8), 993–1013.

Aldrich, H. E. (1979). *Organizations and environments*. Prentice Hall.

Amiri, N. A. I., Eladwiah, R., Rahim, A., & Ahmed, G. (2020). Leadership styles and organizational knowledge management activities: A systematic review Gadjah Mada. *International Journal of Business, 22*(3), 250–275.

Anderson, P. (1999). Perspective: Complexity theory and organization science. *Organization Science, 10*(3), 216–232. https://doi.org/10.1287/orsc.10.3.216

Anderson, S. (2014). The end of publicness? Public and private healthcare organizations are alike in all important respects. *International Journal of Public and Private Healthcare Management and Economics, 3*(3), 44–61.

Andrews, R., Boyne, G. A., & Walker, R. M. (2011). Dimensions of publicness and organizational performance: A review of the evidence. *Journal of Public Administration Research Theory, 21*, 301–319.

Anjaria, K. (2020). Negation and entropy: Effectual knowledge management equipment for learning organizations. *Expert Systems with Applications, 157*(4), 1–23.

Antonelli, G., Mollona, E., & Moschera, L. (2018). Burt-Or Coleman-type rents, or a bit of both? Knowledge management strategies in suppliers' networks. *International Journal of Business and Management, 13*(12), 274–290. https://doi.org/10.5539/ijbm.v13n12p274

Atapattu, M. M., & Huybers, T. (2021). Motivational antecedents, employee engagement and knowledge management performance. *Journal of Knowledge Management, 26*(3), 528–547.

Atkinson, J. (1984). Manpower strategies for flexible organizations. *Personnel Management*.

Aulich, C. (2011). It's not ownership that matters: It's publicness. *Policy Studies, 32*(3), 199–213.

Bagguley, P. (1989). *The post-Fordism enigma: Theories of labour flexibility*. Lancaster Regionalism Group, Lancaster University.

Balde, M., Ferreira, A. I., & Maynard, T. (2018). SECI driven creativity: The role of team trust and intrinsic motivation. *Journal of Knowledge Management, 22*(8), 1688–1711.

Baldwin, C. Y. (2012). Organization design for business ecosystems. *Journal of Organization Design, 1*(1), 20–23.

Baligh, H. H., & Burton, R. M. (1982). The movable boundaries between organizations and markets. *International Journal of Policy Analysis and Information Systems, 6*(4), 435–449.

Berman, S., & Marshall, A. (2014). The next digital transformation: From an individual centered to an everyone-to-everyone economy. *Strategy & Leadership, 42*(5), 9–17. https://doi.org/10.1108/SL-07-2014-0048

Berraies, S. (2020). Effect of middle managers' cultural intelligence on firms' innovation performance: Knowledge sharing as mediator and collaborative climate as moderator. Personnel Review, 49(4), 1015–1038.

Berraies, S., & Chouiref, A. (2022). Exploring the effect of team climate on knowledge management in teams through team work engagement: Evidence from knowledge-intensive firms. *Journal of Knowledge Management, 27*(3), 842–869. https://doi.org/10.1108/JKM-09-2021-0720

Boamah, F. A., Zhang, J., Wen, D., Sherani, M., Hayat, A., & Horbanenko, O. (2022). Enablers of knowledge management: Practical research-based in the construction industry. *International Journal of Innovation Science, 14*(1), 121–137.

Bogason, P. (1998). Changes in the Scandinavian model. From bureaucratic command to inter—organizational negotiation. *Public Administration, 76*(2), 335–354.

Bohanec, M., Robnik-Šikonja, M., & Kljajić, M. (2017). Decision-making framework with double-loop learning through interpretable black-box machine learning models. *Industrial Management & Data Systems, 117*(7), 1389–1406. https://doi.org/10.1108/IMDS-09-2016-0409

Bonazzi, G. (1984). *Storia del pensiero organizzativo*. Franco Angeli.

Bonti, C., & Cori, E. (2012). Clima organizzativo e apprendimento relazionale. In G. Padroni (a cura di), L'ICT nelle dinamiche organizzative delle imprese, Aracne, Roma.

Boulding, K. E. (1953). *The organizational revolution*. Harper & Brothers.
Bourgeois, L. J. (1980). Strategy and environment: A conceptual integration. *Academy of Management Review, 5*(1), 25–39. https://doi.org/10.5465/amr.1980.4288844
Brown, S. L., & Eisenhardt, K. M. (1997). The art of continuous change: Linking complexity theory and time-paced evolution in relentlessly shifting organizations. *Administrative Science Quarterly, 40*(1), 1–34. https://doi.org/10.2307/2393807
Brozovic, D. (2018). Strategic flexibility: A review of the literature. *International Journal of Management Reviews, 20*, 3–31. https://doi.org/10.1111/ijmr.12111
Burton, R. M. (2013). The future of organization design: An interpretative synthesis in three themes. *Journal of Organization Design, 2*(1), 42–44.
Butera, F. (1977). La divisione del lavoro in fabbrica. Marsilio, Venezia.
Butera, F., & Dente, B. (2009). *Change Management nelle Pubbliche Amministrazioni: una proposta*. Franco Angeli.
Cafferata, R. (1984). *Teoria dell'organizzazione: un approccio non contingente*. Franco Angeli.
Cafferata, R. (1986). *Economia delle imprese pubbliche*. Franco Angeli.
Calabrese, M., Iandolo, F., Caputo, F., & Sarno, D. (2018). From mechanical to cognitive view: The changes of decision making in business environment. In S. Barile, M. Pellicano, & F. Polese (Eds.), *Social dynamics in a systems perspective. New economic windows*. Springer. https://doi.org/10.1007/978-3-319-61967-5_12
Canonico, P., De Nito, E., & Mangia, G. (2012). Control mechanisms and knowledge integration in project teams. A case study from the coal fired power plant industry. *Journal of Knowledge Management, 16*(4), 538–554. https://doi.org/10.1108/13673271211246121
Canonico, P., De Nito, E., Esposito, V., Pezzillo Iacono, M., & Consiglio, S. (2020). Knowledge creation in the automotive industry: Analysing obeya-oriented practices using the SECI model. *Journal of Business Research, 112*, 450–457. https://doi.org/10.1016/j.jbusres.2019.11.047
Casalino, N. (2008). Gestione del cambiamento e produttività nelle aziende pubbliche. Metodi e strumenti innovativi, Casucci editore, Bari.
Child, J. (2005). *Organization*. Oxford University Press.
Citroen, C. L. (2011). The role of information in strategic decision-making. *International Journal of Information Management, 31*(6), 493–501. https://doi.org/10.1016/j.ijinfomgt.2011.02.005
Clegg, S. (1990). *Modern organizations: Organization studies in a postmodern world*. Sage.
Cohen, M. D., March, J. G., & Olsen, J. P. (1972). A garbage can model of organizational choice. *Administrative Science Quarterly, 17*, 1–25.
Costa, G., Gubitta, P., & Pittino, D. (2016). *Organizzazione aziendale. Mercati, gerarchie e convenzioni*. McGraw-Hill.
Crook, S., Pakulski, J., & Waters, M. (1992). *Postmodernization: Change in advanced society*. Sage.
Daft, R. L., Murphy, J., & Willmott, H. (2020). *Organization theory & design: An international perspective*. (4th ed.), Cengage Learning EMEA, Southwestern.
Denison, D. R. (1996). What is the difference between organizational culture and organizational climate? A native's point of view on a decade of paradigm wars. *Academy of Management Review, 21*(3), 619–654. https://doi.org/10.5465/amr.1996.9702100310
Diefenbach, T., & Sillince, J. A. A. (2011). Formal and informal hierarchy in different types of organization. *Organization Studies, 32*(11), 1515–1537. https://doi.org/10.1177/0170840611421254
Dobrajska, M., Billinger, S., & Karim, S. (2015). Delegation within hierarchies: How information processing and knowledge characteristics influence the allocation of formal and real decision authority. *Organization Science, 26*(3), 687–704. https://doi.org/10.1287/orsc.2014.0954
Duncan, R. B. (1972). Characteristics of organizational environments and perceived environmental uncertainty. *Administrative Science Quarterly, 17*(3), 313–327.
Eisenhardt, K. M., & Zbaracki, M. J. (1992). Strategic decision making. *Strategic Management Journal, 13*, 17–37. https://doi.org/10.1002/smj.4250130904
Elbanna, S. (2006). Strategic decision-making: Process perspectives. *International Journal of Management Reviews, 8*, 1–20. https://doi.org/10.1111/j.1468-2370.2006.00118.x

Elfenbein, H. A. (1998). Emotion in organizations: A review and theoretical integration. *Academy of Management Annals, 1*(1), 315–386.

Etzioni, A. (1999). Normative-affective factors: Toward a new decision-making model. In *Essays in socio-economics. Studies in economic ethics and philosophy*. Springer. https://doi.org/10.1007/978-3-662-03900-7_5

Etzioni, A. (1961). *Complex organizations*. Free Press.

Fait, M., Cillo, V., Papa, A., Meissner, D., & Scorrano, P. (2021). The roots of 'volunteer' employees' engagement: The silent role of intellectual capital in knowledge-sharing intentions. *Journal of Intellectual Capital, 24*(5), 1–31.

Fischer, B., Salles-Filho, S., Zeitoum, C., & Colugnati, F. (2021). Performance drivers in knowledge intensive entrepreneurial firms: A multidimensional perspective. *Journal of Knowledge Management, 26*(5), 1–17.

Foss, N. J. (2003). Selective intervention and internal hybrids: Interpreting and learning from the rise and decline of the Oticon Spaghetti organization. *Organization Science, 14*(3), 331–349. https://doi.org/10.1287/orsc.14.3.331.15166

Frenkel, S. J. (2003). The embedded character of workplace relations. *Work and Occupations, 30*(2), 135–153. https://doi.org/10.1177/0730888403251516

Frenkel, S. J., Korczynski, M., Tam, M., & Shire, K. (1998). Beyond bureaucracy? Work organization in call centres. *International Journal of Human Resource Management, 9*, 957–979.

Gabel, T. J., & Tokarski, C. (2014). Big data and organizational design: Key challenges await the survey research firm. *Journal of Organization Design, 3*(1), 37–45.

Gorz, A. (1999). Reclaiming work. Polity, Cambridge.

Grandori, A. (1999). Organizzazione e comportamento economico. Il Mulino, Bologna.

Hakonsson, D. D., Eskildsen, J. K., Argote, L., Monster, D., Burton, R. M., & Obel, B. (2016). Exploration versus exploitation: Emotions and performance as antecedents and consequences of team decisions. *Strategic Management Journal, 37*(6), 985–1001. https://doi.org/10.1002/smj.2380

Hancock, P., & Tyler, M. (2001). *Work, post-modernism and organization*. Sage.

Handy, C. (1989). *The age of paradox*. Harvard Business School Press.

Hartmut, R. (2013). *7. Acceleration and growth: External drivers of social acceleration. Social acceleration: A new theory of modernity* (pp. 160–194). Columbia University Press. https://doi.org/10.7312/rosa14834-011

Hecksher, C., & Donnellon, A. (1994). *The post-bureaucratic organization: New perspectives on organizational change*. Sage.

Hedelin, L., & Allwood, C. M. (2002). IT and strategic decision making. *Industrial Management & Data Systems, 102*(3), 125–139. https://doi.org/10.1108/02635570210421318

Henttonen, K., Kianto, A., & Ritala, P. (2016). Knowledge sharing and individual work performance: An empirical study of a public sector organization. *Journal of Knowledge Management, 20*(4), 749–768.

Heydebrand, R. (1989). New organizational forms. *Work and Occupations, 16*(3), 323–357. https://doi.org/10.1177/0730888489016003004

Holmstrom, B., & Roberts, J. (1998). The boundaries of the firm revisited. *Journal of Economic Perspectives, 12*(4), 73–94. https://doi.org/10.1257/jep.12.4.73

Hull, C. E., & Covin, J. G. (2010). Learning capability, technological parity, and innovation mode use. *Journal of Product Innovation Management, 27*, 97–114. https://doi.org/10.1111/j.1540-5885.2009.00702.x

Imam, H., & Zaheer, M. K. (2021). Shared leadership and project success: The roles of knowledge sharing, cohesion and trust in the team. *International Journal of Project Management, 39*(5), 463–473.

Jiang, X., Flores, H. R., Leelawong, R., & Manz, C. C. (2016). The effect of team empowerment on team performance: A cross-cultural perspective on the mediating roles of knowledge sharing and intra-group conflict. *International Journal of Conflict Management, 27*(1), 62–87.

Johnson, P., Wood, G., Brewster, C., & Brookes, M. (2009). The rise of post-bureaucracy: Theorists' fancy or organizational praxis? *International Sociology, 24*(1), 37–61. https://doi.org/10.1177/0268580908100246

Jones, G. (2013). *Organization theory, design and change*. Pearson Education.

Kalleberg, A. L. (2003). Flexible firms and labor market segmentation: Effects of workplace restructuring on jobs and workers. *Work and Occupations, 30*(2), 154–175. https://doi.org/10.1177/0730888403251683

Kanter, R. M. (1989). *When giants learn to dance: Mastering the challenges of strategy, management and careers in the 1990s*. Unwin Hyman.

Kim, W., & Park, J. (2017). Examining structural relationships between work engagement, organizational procedural justice, knowledge sharing, and innovative work behavior for sustainable organizations. *Sustainability, 9*(2), 1–20.

Klahr, D., & Kotovsky, K. (Eds.). (2013). *Complex information processing: The impact on Herbert A. Simon*. Psychology Press.

Koohang, A., Paliszkiewicz, J., & Goluchowski, J. (2017). The impact of leadership on trust, knowledge management, and organizational performance: A research model. *Industrial Management & Data Systems, 117*(3), 521–537.

Kotler, J. P. (2000). *Marketing management: The millennium edition*. Prentice Hall.

Kumar, K. (1995). *From post-industrial to post-modern society*. Blackwell.

Larsen, M. M., Manning, S., & Pederson, T. (2013). Uncovering the hidden costs of offshoring: The interplay of complexity, organizational design and experience. *Strategic Management Journal, 34*(5), 533–552. https://doi.org/10.1002/smj.2023

Liedtka, J., King, A., & Bennett, K. (2013). *Solving problems with design thinking. 10 stories of what works*. Columbia Business School Publishing.

Livijn, M. (2019). Navigating in a hierarchy: How middle managers adapt macro design. *Journal of Organization Design, 8*(7).

Marabelli, M., Rajola, F., Frigerio, C., & Newell, S. (2013). Managing knowledge in large-scale virtual projects: A community-based approach. *International Journal of Managing Projects in Business, 6*(2), 310–331. https://doi.org/10.1108/17538371311319043

March, J. G. (1991). Exploration and exploitation in organizational learning. *Organization Science, 2*(1), 909–923.

Martinez, M. (2004). Organizzazione, informazioni, tecnologie. Il Mulino, Bologna.

Martinez, M., Di Nauta, P., & Sarno, D. (2017). Real and apparent changes of organizational processes in the era of big data analytics. *Studi Organizzativi, 2*, 91–107.

Martini, I., Lasmi, N., Jaya, N., & Sutrisni, N. (2017). Improving cooperative performance through human resource development efforts. *International Journal of Social Sciences and Humanities (IJSSH), 1*(3), 49–58. https://doi.org/10.21744/ijssh.v1i3.55

McAuley, J., Duberley, J., Johnson, P., Sorrentino, M., & Levi, S. (2017). Organizzazione Aziendale. Concetti, teorie, applicazioni. Pearson, United Kingdom.

Meek, C. B. (2004). The dark side of Japanese management in the 1990s: Karoshi and ijime in the Japanese workplace. *Journal of Managerial Psychology, 19*(3), 312–331. https://doi.org/10.1108/02683940410527775

Mercurio, R. (2016). *Organizational networks for innovation*. Egea.

Mercurio, R., & Martinez, M. (2009). *Modelli di governance e processi di cambiamento nelle public utilities*. Franco Angeli.

Miles, R. E. (1965). Human relations or human resources? *Harvard Business Review, 43*(4), 148–158.

Miles, R. E. (1975). *Theories of management*. McGraw Hill.

Miles, R. E., & Snow, C. C. (1978). *Organizational strategy. Structure and process*. McGraw-Hill.

Min, J., Lee, J., Ryu, S., & Lee, H. (2021). The effects of interaction between team climates and KMS value perception on knowledge activities: A multilevel socio-technical systems approach. *Information Technology and Management, 23*(1), 1–18.

Mintzberg, H., Raisinghani, D., & Theoret, A. (1976). The structure of unstructured decision processes. *Administrative Science Quarterly, 21*, 246–227.

Morelli, C. (2017). L'architettura organizzativa e gli schemi generali aziendali. In G. Rebora (Ed.), *Scienza dell'organizzazione. Il design di strutture, processi e ruoli*. Carocci.

Muhammed, S., & Zaim, H. (2020). Peer knowledge sharing and organizational performance: The role of leadership support and knowledge management success. *Journal of Knowledge Management, 24*(10), 2455–2489.

Nezafati, N., Razaghi, S., Moradi, H., Shokouhyar, S., & Jafari, S. (2023). Promoting knowledge sharing performance in a knowledge management system: Do knowledge workers' behavior patterns matter? *VINE Journal of Information and Knowledge Management Systems, 53*(4), 637–662. https://doi.org/10.1108/VJIKMS-11-2020-0202

Nohria, N., & Berkley, J. (1994). The virtual organization: Bureaucracy, technology and the implosion of control. In C. Hecksher & A. Donnellon (Eds.), *The post-bureaucratic organization: New perspectives on organizational change*. Sage.

Ouchi, W. (1981). *Theory Z: How American business can meet the Japanese challenge*. Addison Wesley.

Parsons, T. (1960). *Structure and process in modern societies*. The Free Press.

Piore, M., & Sabel, C. (1994). *The second industrial divide: Possibilities for prosperity*. Basic Books.

Polanyi, M. (1966). *The tacit dimension*. Routledge and Kegan Paul.

Pollert, A. (1988). Dismantling flexibility. *Capital and Class, 34*, 42–75.

Pollert, A. (1991). The orthodoxy of flexibility. In A. Pollert (Ed.), *Farewell to flexibility*. Blackwell.

Rainey, H. G., Backoff, R., & Levine, C. (1976). Comparing public and private organizations. *Public Administration Review, 36*, 233–244.

Rebora, G. (2017). *Scienza dell'Organizzazione*. Carocci.

Rickards, T., & Clark, M. (2012). *Dilemmas of leadership*. Routledge.

Robbins, S. P. (1990). *Organization theory: Structure, design and applications*. Prentice Hall.

Robinson, D. T. (2008). Strategic alliances and the boundaries of the firm. *Review of Financial Studies, 21*(2), 649–681. https://doi.org/10.1093/rfs/hhm084

Rofiaty, R. (2019). The relational model of entrepreneurship and knowledge management toward innovation, strategy implementation and improving Islamic boarding school performance. *Journal of Modelling in Management, 14*(3), 662–685.

Rožman, M., & Štrukelj, T. (2024). A multidimensional model for implementing knowledge management in an enterprise to increase employee motivation and Enterprise's competitiveness. In M. Valeri (Ed.), *Knowledge management and knowledge sharing. Business strategies and an emerging theoretical field*. Springer.

Sahibzada, U. F., Latif, K. F., Xu, Y., & Khalid, R. (2020). Catalyzing knowledge management processes towards knowledge worker satisfaction: Fuzzy-set qualitative comparative analysis. *Journal of Knowledge Management, 24*(10), 2373–2400.

Sarti, D., & Torre, T. (2018). Reward management in small-medium knowledge-intensive firms. Evidence from Italy. In S. Perkins (Ed.), *The Routledge companion to reward management*. Routledge.

Selznick, P. (1964). Foundations of the theory of organization. In A. Litterer (Ed.), *Organizations, structure and behavior*. Wiley.

Shepherd, N. G., & Rudd, J. M. (2014). Context in strategic decision-making. *International Journal of Management Reviews, 16*, 340–364. https://doi.org/10.1111/ijmr.12023

Siggelkow, N., & Rivkin, J. (2005). Speed and search: Designing organizations for turbulence and complexity. *Organization Science, 16*(2), 101–122. https://doi.org/10.1287/orsc.1050.0116

Simon, H. A. (1947). *Administrative behavior*. Harper & Row.

Simon, H. A. (1967). *The architecture of complexity*. MIT Press.

Simon, H. A. (1960). *The new science of management decision*. Harper.

Skorstad, E. G. (2009a). The ambiguity of flexibility. In E. G. Skorstad & H. Ramsdal (Eds.), *Flexible organizations and the new working life: A European perspective*. Ashgate Publishing.

Skorstad, E. G. (2009b). Concluding remarks: The complex dynamics of the flexible company. In E. G. Skorstad & H. Ramsdal (Eds.), *Flexible organizations and the new working life: A European perspective*. Ashgate Publishing.

Sorenson, O., Rivkin, J., & Fleming, L. (2004). Complexity, networks and knowledge flow. *Research Policy, 33*(10), 1615–1634. https://doi.org/10.1016/j.respol.2006.05.002

Stinchcombe, A. L. (1965). Social structure and organizations. In J. G. March (Ed.), *Handbook od organizations*. Rand Mc Nally & Co.

Sy, T., & Coté, S. (2004). Emotional intelligence: A key ability to succeed in the matrix organization. *Journal of Management Development, 23*(5), 437–455. https://doi.org/10.1108/02621710410537056

Tagiuri, R., & Litwin, G. H. (1968). *Organizational climate*. Harvard University Press.

Taylor, F. W. (1911). *The principles of scientific management*. Harper & Brothers.

Thompson, P., & McHugh, D. (2009). *Work organizations: A critical introduction*. Palgrave MacMillan.

Valeri, M. (2021). *Organizational studies. Implications for the strategic management*. Springer.

Valeri, M. (2024). *Knowledge management and knowledge sharing. Business strategies and an emerging theoretical field*. Springer. https://doi.org/10.1007/978-3-031-37868-3

Van Zandt, T. (1999). Real-time decentralized information processing as a model of organizations with Boundedly rational agents. *Review of Economic Studies, 66*(3), 633–658. https://doi.org/10.1111/1467-937X.00101

Vidal, M. (2007). Lean production, worker empowerment, and job satisfaction: A qualitative analysis and critique. *Critical Sociology, 33*(1–2), 247–278. https://doi.org/10.1163/156916307X168656

Walker, R. M., & Bozeman, B. (2011). Publicness and organizational performance. *Journal of Public Administration Research and Theory, 21*(3), 279–281.

Wei, Y., & Miraglia, S. (2017). Organizational culture and knowledge transfer in project-based organizations: Theoretical insights from a Chinese construction firm. *International Journal of Project Management, 35*(4), 571–585.

Weick, K., & Berlinger, L. (1989). Career improvisations in self-designing organizations. In M. Arthur & B. Lawrence (Eds.), *Handbook of career theory*. Cambridge University Press.

Wood, S. (1989). *The transformation of work?* Unwin Hyman.

Xue, Y., Bradley, J., & Liang, H. (2011). Team climate, empowering leadership and knowledge sharing. *Journal of Knowledge Management, 15*(2), 299–312.

Yao, J., Liu, X., & He, W. (2021). How to make use of team knowledge variety? The role of power disparity. *Journal of Knowledge Management, 26*(3), 722–742.

Yin, J., Ma, Z., Yu, H., Jia, M., & Liao, G. (2020). Transformational leadership and employee knowledge sharing: Explore the mediating roles of psychological safety and team efficacy. *Journal of Knowledge Management, 24*(2), 150–171.

Zhang, X., & Wang, X. (2021). Team learning in interdisciplinary research teams: Antecedents and consequences. *Journal of Knowledge Management, 25*(6), 1429–1455.

Zhang, X., Wang, X., & Zhao, W. (2020). Social capital and knowledge integration in interdisciplinary research teams: A multilevel analysis. *Management Decision, 59*(8), 1972–1989.

Zhao, L., & Detlor, B. (2021). Towards a contingency model of knowledge sharing: Interaction between social capital and social exchange theories. *Knowledge Management Research & Practice, 26*, 1–19.

Zhou, K. Z., & Wu, F. (2010). Technological capability, strategic flexibility, and product innovation. *Strategic Management Journal, 31*, 547–561. https://doi.org/10.1002/smj.830

Complexity and Knowledge 2

2.1 Complexity in Organization: A Systemic Approach

Organizational complexity has consistently driven corporate governance to adopt strategies and approaches that are essential for the organization's survival in the challenging environment it engages with, which ultimately influences its successes or crises (Dooley, 2002; Moldoveanu & Bauer, 2004).

In today's world, organizations operate within a socioeconomic environment shaped by globalization, the necessity to modernize national systems, and the rapid pace of technological advancements. Organizations face increasing competitive pressures that compel them to contend with emerging rivals and new competition regulations. The organization encounters two opposing requirements: firstly, the necessity to tailor its offerings to meet the increasingly varied demands of the market and, secondly, the aim to achieve economies of scale to reduce production costs in response to intense global competitive pressure.

The dynamics of technological innovation are becoming more intricate: initially, significant breakthroughs that represented a clear departure from previous practices were succeeded by phases of stability to facilitate their integration into the market (Narvekar & Jain, 2006; Nieto, 2004).

The idea of complexity has been examined by numerous researchers (Horn, 2008; Manson, 2001; Phelan, 2001). Each has infused the idea of complexity with an air of uncertainty, leading to countless definitions, to the extent that they express a desire to establish a physical-mathematical theory concerning complexity.

The complexity that Fordism managed to govern today explodes and becomes an uncontrollable phenomenon. The increasingly differentiated needs of consumers force the organization to offer a wide range of products. The life cycle of products tends to become increasingly shorter, and today's managers therefore find themselves making decisions that contribute to multiplying speed and variability.

M. Valeri, *Organizations and Knowledge Management*, Knowledge Management and Organizational Learning 16, https://doi.org/10.1007/978-3-031-97954-5_2

The increasing complexity of the environment signals both the failure of a cognitive framework grounded in cause-and-effect relationships and the shift from the modern era to the postmodern era, enabling the exploration of a more dynamic and diverse reality.

The rise of intricate phenomena marked by diverse elements and their interconnections necessitates a shift in approach. This new perspective focuses not on simplifying reality but on comprehending its complexity.

The organization's ability to manage the intricacies brought about by solely mechanical production has increasingly highlighted the essential appreciation of information and knowledge that depends on human intelligence, which is no longer purely mechanized or scientific. On the one hand, we are observing a significant transformation in corporate culture that shifts from viewing the organization as a machine reliant on calculation and abstract knowledge for strategic decisions to perceiving it as an evolving organism closely connected to its environment, the knowledge it possesses, and the learning abilities of its resources.

Conversely, the organization is experiencing growth, which can be linked to the rising specialization among organizations and the advancement of networks.

Ultimately, we are observing the emergence of new economies driven by the technological revolution associated with the extensive utilization of information technologies. This not only transforms the way knowledge is disseminated but also significantly speeds up changes in traditional supply structures and alters the methods of operation within purchasing and consumption systems (Lebel & Lorek, 2009).

The phenomenon of complexity can be analyzed based on three dimensions: *variety, variability, and indeterminacy* (Klir, 1985; Iván Tarride, 2013; Alhadeff-Jones, 2008).

Variety is identified in the possible variations with which the phenomenon presents itself to the eyes of the observer. The distinct components that make up a phenomenon can appear differently to the observer, who may possess either full or limited understanding of them. The governing body thus possesses an understanding of the phenomenon that differs based on both the diversity of characteristics and the quantity and quality of the phenomenal attributes.

Variability is identified in the further variety which, with the passage of time, can emerge and add to the preexisting one. Variety pertains to the diversity of potential instances, while variability indicates the chance that an event exhibits successive changes over time.

Indeterminacy manifests itself in the ability to understand the phenomenon in its entirety. Indeterminacy represents a watershed between awareness and complexity and the rationality of governing it. On the one hand, the governing body realizes the difficulty of learning the phenomenon due to its variety; on the other hand, it tries to understand it by trying to govern the variety.

The idea of complexity is associated not just with the numerous vertical and horizontal components that make up an organization but also with the various occupational and professional specialties within the organizational framework that carry out specific tasks. These tasks are informed by the knowledge gained from experience and the roles they fulfill (Richards et al., 2019).

It is important to emphasize that the organization consists not only of components but also of individuals who integrate professionalism and special skills, thereby adding layers of complexity to its nature through their personal emotions. This occurs both when they behave in ways that contradict the institution's objectives, leading to conflicts that must be addressed, and when they make choices that are not always reasonable.

Over the years, several factors have played a role in heightening the complexity of the relationship between the organization and its environment. The alterations brought about by these elements, along with the diverse strategic approaches taken by firms to establish their presence in the market, have resulted in an increase in variability and diversity.

The primary reason for this is the unpredictability that pervades the environment, which has evolved into a dynamic and chaotic state. In uncertain situations, making decisions about investments in production factors with long recovery periods becomes challenging, as does predicting potential future trends in technology, economics, and social dynamics across various markets. To ensure cohesion and integration within the mental framework, the organization is prompted to establish a role in the organizational structure overseen by a human resource who acts as an integrator. This position utilizes a leadership approach that fosters improved communication (both vertical and horizontal) and supports ongoing learning.

An organization aiming for long-term survival encourages creativity and intelligence by promoting responsibility and improving communication between management and employees. This fosters a culture of reflection and skill enhancement and ensures the development of products and production methods that align with market demands.

Every organization develops its own repository of knowledge that it can utilize as needed in particular contexts and at specific times, i.e., within a timeframe that aligns with the stability of the proposed events. The significant demand for a cognitive resource to navigate corporate complexity necessitates a considerable amount of time. Additionally, for knowledge to remain relevant and facilitate effective actions, it must be disseminated through procedures that also take time. Knowledge can also become outdated or invalid over time. Consequently, it is essential to swiftly apply investments into new and appropriate knowledge from a time perspective. The effective coordination of time and knowledge elements will be crucial for facilitating the swift and timely advancement of new insights (Smiraglia, 2014; Primas, 2017).

2.2 Organizational Intuition as a Fundamental Component for Dealing with Complexity

There is a consensus that the success of organizations hinges on governance and management's capacity to establish a streamlined, adaptable, and learning-focused organization. The processes of learning are intricately linked to both individual and collective mental mechanisms that give rise to intelligence. The key elements of an organization's intangible assets include creativity, imagination, inventiveness, inspiration, overall intuition, adaptability, sensitivity, the capacity for perception, and forward-thinking visions.

Jung's research (1929) on personality types has been highly beneficial in illustrating the notable variations in how corporate decision-makers process information during their decision-making activities. The theory of psychological types emerges from extensive research aimed at uncovering the logical characteristics that shape how individuals engage with their surroundings.

The essential variations in personality lead to distinct approaches to understanding the reality around us, assessing potential outcomes, forming judgments, and reaching decisions (Stitzman, 2008). There are two basic ways in which people take in and process information: *sensoriality* and *intuition*.

Sensoriality refers to the modality that favors the five senses in the process of collecting and processing information. Sensoriality emphasizes tangible data and facts, centering on the present moment and what can be seen, felt, and smelled. It aims to assess and measure the likelihood of an occurrence.

Intuition considers the whole rather than the individual parts, grasps the intimate interrelationship, and extrapolates a resulting one. Intuition is oriented to the possibility of the event. Sensory perception focuses on individual parts; intuition overcomes them and goes beyond them.

Regarding the decision-making process, people use two other fundamental modalities: *reflective thinking* and *impression/feeling* (Pappas, 2016).

Reflective mode favors objectivity, analysis, logic, and reasoning. *Impression/feeling mode* is subjective and is absolutely nonanalytical.

Given that organizations are viewed as a collective of individuals, it is evident that some organizations emphasize the sensory dimension, while others prioritize the intuitive dimension. The logical-sensory structure is typically characterized by a cold, highly organized, and hierarchical approach. In this framework, rules are paramount, and significant emphasis is placed on task allocation while taking functional specialization into account.

The number remains unchanged. It is an organization tasked with handling a vast amount of data and envisioning the future as an extension of the past and present. There is an inclination to appreciate what is difficult and to value experience. In this type of organization, management cycle is fully executed, which includes planning, organizing, programming, and controlling. On the other hand, in a more intuitive organization, the importance of interpersonal relationships is emphasized.

It lacks a formal structure, yet often it resembles a network configuration. It is an organization that possesses a clear vision and a defined sense of purpose and mission, driven by the belief that the future can be shaped.

In this context, creativity and intuition are held in high regard, as efforts are made to strike an appropriate balance between the tangible and intangible elements, with remaining unchanged. It is challenging to provide one definitive explanation of the idea of intuition (Dollinger et al., 2004; Samier, 2018; Akpur, 2024).

Occasionally, this idea is misused in modern language. Intuition appears to be a common skill that varies among individuals. Intuition relates to multidisciplinary because it is a complex phenomenon that necessitates an analytical approach across various levels. Intuition aids in achieving an appropriate equilibrium between the external world and internal perceptions, enabling effective management of complexity, uncertainty, and conflict.

Intuition represents a type of intelligence that cannot be reached through mere logical thought. The human mind is truly remarkable; once it grasps an idea or comprehends a concept, it expands and does not revert to its original size. It seems boundless, with immense possibilities.

Multiple definitions of intelligence have been given which are not always reconcilable. In general, *structural* definitions of intelligence can be distinguished from *functional* definitions.

Structural definitions tend to capture the basic factors of intelligence. These factors are quantified through statistical processing of some coefficients used in batteries of psycho-aptitude tests to measure different habits. *Functional* definitions of intelligence, on the other hand, tend to capture its ability to adapt to new needs and to highlight the thought processes of antiquarians: man solves a new problem in situations in which neither instinct nor habit comes into play.

The three areas of consciousness to be aware of in order to best develop intuition are (1) *conscious*, (2) *preconscious*, and (3) *subconscious* (Seebohm, 1992).

Conscious is the part of the mind that functions in the waking state: you must be awake to be aware of a certain fact. The conscious mind is capable of focusing on only one thought at a time, even if it takes minimal concentration. When you attempt to manage multiple aspects at once, your mind becomes overwhelmed, leading to tiredness, confusion, frustration, and insecurity.

Preconscious operates in a waking state, but, unlike the conscious, it can range across multiple aspects, if these do not require great concentration. Preconscious mind is capable of handling multiple thoughts, provided that these thoughts are familiar and routine.

Subconscious operates continuously, even while we are sleeping. It pertains to the realm ruled by dreams, fantasies, imagination, and creative activities. The subconscious can mix experiences and impressions in an endless variety of combinations. It is only when these impressions become conscious that constructive work can be done on them, allowing for processing that leads to results.

Subconscious contains an incredible amount of different information, skills, and experiences. Intuition and creativity arise from the subconscious.

The role of intuition and creativity in the growth of organizations is vital. Creativity is not defined by straightforward analytical reasoning; rather, its essence is rooted in the ability to cultivate highly intuitive divergent thinking that can lead to the development of a business idea. In this regard, we are entering a new era of management that emphasizes the success of creativity and intuition in the decision-making process.

2.3 Contribution of the Learning Curve to the Valorization of Knowledge

In management literature, the subject of knowledge has been explored through various concepts that highlight its significance for gaining a competitive edge. In the present economic landscape, knowledge serves as a crucial strategic element needed to navigate complexity. During the 1960's, growing market share served as a key focus for the strategic management of organizations (this mathematical model essentially highlights a negative correlation between experience and the labor hours required to produce product units) (Hladchenko, 2016; Grant & Baden-Fuller, 1995; Lane & Lubatkin, 1998).

In today's environment, however, knowledge has truly supplanted the traditional assets that formed the basis of competitive advantage, and the enhancement of intellectual resources has become an increasingly effective strategic asset upon which to bolster investments, keeping as it is. The growth in knowledge and abilities enables effective management of much of the environmental intricacies (Peteraf, 1993).

Today's organizations encounter every new challenge as if they are beginning afresh in a market that has grown intricate and divided, where making accurate predictions is becoming progressively more challenging.

In today's highly intricate world, the competitive challenge hinges on the accessibility of knowledge, meaning that it is crucial. The successful organization is the one that can unify behaviors, standards, and values across various cultures, nations, and customer bases.

Effective knowledge management enhances the pace of innovation, shortens the time required to bring products to market, facilitates the development of new business opportunities, and accelerates the acquisition of data and information (Kogut & Zander, 1992; Polanyi, 1958).

The organization's engagement with its dynamic surroundings helps not only in leveraging existing knowledge from its intellectual foundations but also in generating new insights by acquiring and exchanging both behavioral and technological innovations, as well as navigating the unpredictable aspects of the environment. The greater the organization's quantitative and qualitative knowledge levels, which motivate it to interact with its environment in pursuit of equilibrium, the better it can minimize the complexity gap and progress toward evolution.

In this context, it is important to emphasize certain limitations that have been identified in the managerial literature regarding organizations' learning curves, which remain unaddressed. To begin with, it is uncertain how an organization's experience exhibits traits of repetition and accumulation, which are fundamental to traditional learning curves. Specifically, the factors that facilitate the transfer of knowledge across various decision-making scenarios and environmental settings have not been addressed (Glock et al., 2019; Dar-EI, 2000).

Moreover, relying on the total production volume as the primary factor explaining organizations' efficiency improvements seems deceptive and hinders any consideration of the ways in which organizations internalize this information and convert it into more efficient practices. Ultimately, it remains unclear why there is such a significant variation in learning rates, both among organizations from different industries and among those operating within the same competitive landscape with similar technologies.

As a result, the experience curve does not adequately capture how organizations can enhance their tendency to leverage the knowledge acquired.

2.4 Knowledge Hierarchy Model

According to Bratianu and Bejinaru (2023), the widely recognized knowledge pyramid, also referred to as the wisdom pyramid, serves as an effective analogy for grasping the fundamental ideas of data, information, knowledge, and wisdom (DIKW) along with their transitions.

Figure 2.1 illustrates a simplified version of a highly intricate and largely uncharted process, which is shaped by each person's education, experience, intelligence, and cultural background while retaining as it is. Although we can identify four levels of understanding complexity, these levels vary from person to person. Furthermore, it is essential to note that every level is defined by varying degrees of richness and intensity in understanding, influenced by the contextual experiences and organizational settings. The shift from knowledge to wisdom involves the processes of judgment and making decisions. Consequently, wisdom encompasses far more than just knowledge, as it also involves judgment.

The knowledge hierarchy serves as a significant model for comprehending the primary tiers of understanding and the growing intricacy of knowledge processing from the base of the pyramid to its apex, although its importance should not be exaggerated. Furthermore, it is crucial to illustrate the progression involved in each shift: from data to information, from information to knowledge, and from knowledge to wisdom. These changes are not linear and are considerably more intricate than what a straightforward hierarchy might imply.

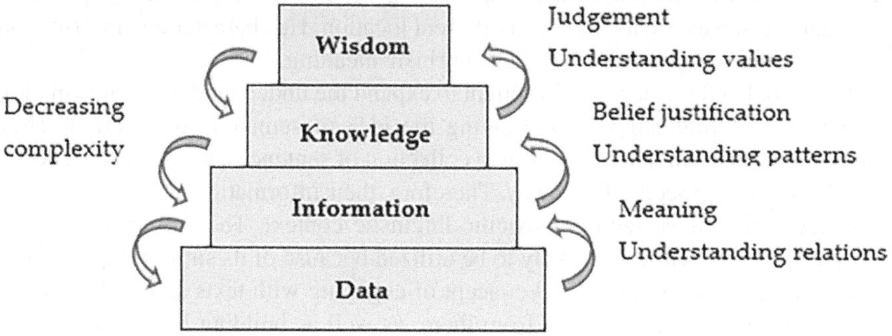

Fig. 2.1 The DIKW hierarchy. *Source*: Bratianu and Bejinaru (2023)

Data

Data illustrates the information at the primary tier of the hierarchy, consisting of letters, digits, symbols, or various combinations of these elements. As suggested by Davenport and Prusak (2000, p. 2), "Data is a set of discrete, objective facts about events. In an organizational context, data is most usefully described as structured records of transactions." Data holds no intrinsic meaning on its own. It serves as the foundational material for information. If we come across a table filled with numbers that lacks a title, we cannot determine how to understand them. The advent of advanced intelligent technologies has led to a significant surge in the volume, diversity, and speed of data, growing at an exponential rate that traditional management methods and tools cannot effectively manage. Big data, predictive analytics, and data science have developed into distinct fields dedicated to managing the vast amounts of data, investigating potential correlations among variables, and generating insights from this information (McAfee & Brynjolfsson, 2012).

Information

The idea of information serves as the essential foundation of the entire knowledge hierarchy due to its semantic aspects derived from mathematics, information science, linguistics, philosophy, and management.

Shannon (1948) created a mathematical framework for communication to address challenges in engineering communication systems when faced with external disturbances. To simplify matters, Shannon analyzed a general communication system made up of several parts: (a) a sender responsible for creating messages intended for transmission; (b) a transmitter, which is a technological apparatus that converts the message into a format of electrical or electromagnetic signals; (c) a receiver, which is a technological device capable of converting the incoming signals into audio, video, or a combination of both; (d) the end user, who interprets the messages received; and (e) an external source of disturbances. The engineering challenge outlined by Shannon involved creating the ability to precisely replicate a message chosen at one location at a different location. He characterized information as a mathematical construct that lacks intrinsic meaning.

Bar-Hillel and Carnap (1953) sought to expand the understanding of information in the field of linguistics by presenting the idea of semantic information. They viewed a generic language as a limited collection of sentences, where each sentence is utilized with a specific frequency. Therefore, their information concept may hold a related significance within a specific linguistic context. The authors created an advanced theory that was unlikely to be utilized because of its simplifying assumptions. However, the fundamental concept of engaging with texts and seeking ways to extract semantic information from them, as well as building high-quality databases, continues to pose a challenge for information technology professionals.

In knowledge management, the term *information* is characterized in relation to the ideas of data and knowledge (Allen, 2017; Liew, 2013; Rowley, 2007; Jashapara,

2011). The shift from data to information can be achieved by taking into account a semantic framework and a range of relationships between the data and that framework. Nonetheless, it is not merely a straightforward process of adding but rather an analysis of data processing within the context of a semantic framework. Individuals interpret data through the mental frameworks they have formed via education and personal experiences (Senge, 1999). Due to this process, information is endowed with significance and importance (Jashapara, 2011; Ackoff, 1989; Choo, 2006) in relation to a specific context.

From a computational standpoint, Davenport and Prusak (2000) demonstrated that information arises from data through several processes, including contextualization, categorization, computation, correction, and condensation.

Knowledge

Within the DIKW hierarchy, the idea of knowledge occupies the primary role (Nonaka & Takeuchi, 1995; Jashapara, 2011; Davenport & Prusak, 2000). Polanyi (1983) made a significant impact on transforming that paradigm by highlighting the role of perception in the learning process and defining the tacit dimension of knowledge. In this way, Polanyi incorporated experiential knowledge into the learning process and emphasized the distinction between knowledge that can be articulated through natural or symbolic language and knowledge that can only be conveyed through nonverbal communication.

Nonaka and Takeuchi (1995) formulated the theory of knowledge-creating dynamics focusing on the relationship between explicit and tacit knowledge. Tacit knowledge refers to the personal understanding gained from hands-on experience, which is managed by the subconscious cognitive aspects of the brain. It can manifest directly through body language and is converted into explicit knowledge by utilizing either a natural or symbolic language (Damasio, 2012; Kolb, 2015; Pinker, 2008; Holden & Glisby, 2010). It is essential to remember this observation when examining the DIKW hierarchy, as it highlights the constraints of that model in generating knowledge through the processing of information. Expanding on this framework, Nonaka and Takeuchi (2019) introduced their model of knowledge creation dynamics (SECI model), which includes four fundamental processes: (a) socialization, (b) externalization, (c) combination, and (d) internalization.

It takes place at the personal level and involves converting important explicit knowledge into tacit knowledge. The four processes form a continuous cycle over time, creating a *knowledge spiral* (Nonaka & Takeuchi, 1995, 2019). It is noteworthy to point out that the SECI model does not have a relationship with the DIKW hierarchy, as information does not need to be viewed as a fundamental resource for knowledge. SECI model has been widely embraced by numerous researchers and practitioners due to its straightforward and intuitive nature. Nonetheless, the model has certain restrictions that must be recognized by individuals engaged in the study and application of knowledge management. There is not a strict theoretical foundation for it, but it can be demonstrated through numerous real-world examples. The

SECI model is particularly relevant to Japanese firms because knowledge sharing is an integral part of Japanese education. In contrast, this practice is less distinctly embraced in cultures characterized by intense individual competition. In those cultures, the prevailing belief is that sharing knowledge is a professional risk, and it should be counterbalanced with the practice of knowledge hiding (Bratianu et al., 2020; Connelly et al., 2012).

Wisdom

The notion of wisdom is significantly more intricate than its placement within the DIKW hierarchy, despite being the highest point of that structure. Wisdom involves acting according to a belief system, reflecting an understanding of spiritual knowledge and the process of making decisions (Jashapara, 2011). While a person's beliefs serve as guiding principles, the process of making decisions is intricate and shaped by various types of knowledge, including rational, emotional, and spiritual, along with the interactions among them (Kahneman, 2011; Bratianu et al., 2021; Gladwell, 2005).

Hall (2010) highlighted a significant characteristic of wisdom—the ability to handle uncertainty and ambiguity arising from a lack of knowledge. The theory of knowledge domains, encompassing rational, emotional, and spiritual insights, is crucial for grasping the intricacies of the concept of wisdom. Furthermore, an individual's ability to navigate uncertainty distinguishes their degree of wisdom. Unpredictability is an inherent aspect of what lies ahead. Hence, wisdom is connected to individuals' ability to think strategically when they are making choices. Indeed, assessing an individual's wisdom is possible after a decision has been taken and we observe the outcomes. This suggests a timeframe and perspective for a potential future. For instance, when individuals become aware of the risk of knowledge loss within an organization, those with a strategic mindset create strategies aimed at preserving knowledge and minimizing the impact of the associated risks. Intergenerational learning is among the most effective approaches for organizations that have multiple layers of different generations (Bratianu & Leon, 2015).

The DIKW hierarchy is regarded as a standard model due to its simplicity and intuitive nature. However, it fails to clarify the mechanisms and driving forces that lead to each transformation from one level to the next in terms of complexity. Furthermore, it fosters the misleading notion that these changes are singular in generating information, knowledge, and wisdom.

Liebowitz (1997, 2000) presented a nine-step approach to knowledge management:

1. Transform information into knowledge
2. Identify and verify knowledge
3. Capture and secure knowledge

4. Organize knowledge
5. Retrieve and apply knowledge
6. Combine knowledge
7. Create knowledge
8. Learn knowledge
9. Distribute/sell knowledge

Overall, a key concern in knowledge management is the structuring, dissemination, and enhancement of knowledge. Knowledge can be produced through data mining tools, obtained from external sources, or can be improved and updated. The gathered information can subsequently be structured by categorizing the knowledge components, sifting through content, and creating connections and relationships between the elements. Subsequently, this information is incorporated into a knowledge base and shared with the decision support applications. The insights gained from the decision support applications are utilized to enhance the present knowledge and provide feedback for knowledge organization.

According to Metaxiotis et al. (2003) the ways knowledge is displayed to the organizational members. Figure 2.2 presents graphically the whole process of knowledge management.

Overall, an organization can develop various methods to structure its knowledge base. Due to varying presentation styles, members within the organization frequently struggle to reorganize, merge, and synthesize knowledge from diverse and separate sources. An additional crucial aspect is the dissemination and sharing of knowledge. When information is exchanged within the organization, it builds up over time. Information technology and the Internet have facilitated and amplified the exchange of knowledge, while emerging technologies can enhance this process even further.

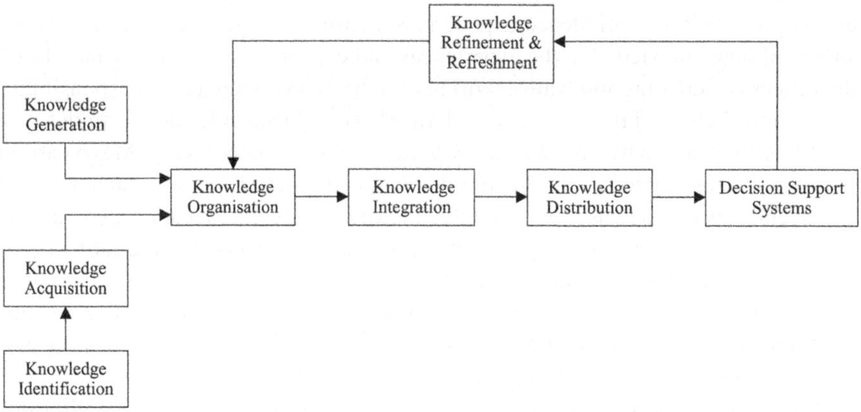

Fig. 2.2 Stage of knowledge processing. *Source:* Metaxiotis et al. (2003)

2.5 Meta-Analysis and Development of Knowledge

Several research approaches, over the years, have explored the concept of knowledge. Among these, we remember:

1. Evolutionary theory of Organization
2. Economic-Managerial Literature
3. Resource Base Theory

The *evolutionary theory* of *organization* originates from the relevance of the concept of change. It hypothesizes an economic situation in which efficient organizations tend to oust marginal ones. From this viewpoint, the organization is viewed as a living organism, with its "genes" consisting of routines that collect the essential knowledge needed for its functioning. Routines shape the growth of the organization. As a result, these skills form the foundation upon which businesses operate and allow them to attain economic success (Rumelt, 1984, 1987; Penrose, 1959).

For Nelson and Winter (1982), routines represent a collective dimension of the possession of knowledge held by organizations. Routines are understood as the set of rules, procedures, and behaviors that are activated in organizations automatically. They are considered genetic material and represent the meta-individual capabilities of organizations. Nelson and Winter highlighted how organizations evolve through changes in management and organizational procedures that occur at a meta-individual level with the inevitable consequence of an increase in the wealth of skills within the organization. In their analysis, Nelson and Winter (1982) underestimated the aspect of the active and subjective creation of new knowledge by economic subjects.

Managerial literature of the last century identifies two currents of study: a scientific orientation which, through the contribution of Taylor (1911) and his followers, arrives at the *scientificization* strategy implementation according to scientific method; the *scientificization* of strategy; it is a managerial approach which considers Mayo (1945) as a privileged exponent. Scientific management failed to grasp a source of new knowledge in the experiences and evaluations of workers and placed the process of creating innovative working methods solely under the responsibility of managers who had the task of considering knowledge as rules and formulas.

While knowledge was not a primary focus in management theory, Mayo carried out several experiments at the Hawthorne plant of Western Electric, which revealed that social aspects such as morale, the feeling of belonging to a team, and an understanding of human behavior positively influenced productivity. Barnard (1938) emphasized that not only knowledge encompasses a logical and linguistic component, but it also involves a behavioral dimension. He further contended that a genuine leader is someone who establishes values, beliefs, and knowledge to strengthen the integrity of the knowledge system within the organization.

According to Barnard, understanding is crucial for exceeding the capabilities of both human cognition and information processing.

Over the years, the study of knowledge in managerial disciplines has been influenced by epistemology, psychology, philosophy, and sociology, that is, concentrated on two fundamental dimensions:

1. The nature of knowledge (tacit and explicit knowledge)
2. The level of knowledge possession (individual and collective dimension of knowledge)

As regards the nature of knowledge, part of the literature agrees in dividing knowledge resources into (a) *codifiable knowledge*, i.e., the set of data, information, or knowledge capable of being codified so that the meaning is objectively attributed, and (b) *non-codifiable knowledge*, i.e., the set of skills and procedures which are difficult to codify because they are the result of a learning process accumulated over time (Argyris, 1977, 1999; Argyris & Schon, 1978).

Nonaka and Takeuchi (1995) discuss on tacit knowledge and implicit knowledge. They believe that the knowledge of business processes represents the fulcrum on which the development of the organization hinges. This understanding is derived from personal and collective learning experiences, and it is disseminated and exchanged because of its explicit or implicit characteristics.

Regarding the level of knowledge possession, the managerial literature identifies a distinction between the levels of knowledge possessed at an individual level and at a group level. Von Hayek (1989) identifies two levels of knowledge possession: (1) knowledge possessed at the personal level or where news and information reside and (2) knowledge possessed at the market level or where all the knowledge distributed among individuals is synthesized. The relationship between the two tiers of knowledge results in a synthesized understanding that contributes to determining the price of the final output, while it remains unchanged. Indeed, this represents significantly different knowledge when compared to the total information held by individuals.

Resource-based theory (Alvarez & Barney, 2000; Barney, 1986, 1991, 2001), despite having the merit of conceptualizing the conditions of sustainability of the competitive advantage of organizations, highlights some limitations:

1. It identifies and statically lists the organization resources necessary to achieve the competitive advantage.
2. Interorganizational learning is a closed process in nature. The theory zeroes in on the individual organization, omitting the potential benefits that could arise from engaging in interactive processes with its surroundings (e.g., outsourcing processes, cooperative relations between organizations, etc.).
3. The theory does not recognize the distinction of the parts that constitute the organization. As a result, it is challenging to identify the roles played by each of the parties involved in generating value (such as the governing body, management framework, and operational framework).
4. There is an asymmetry in the endowment of resources between organizations as they are distributed in a non-heterogeneous manner between them.

5. The success and preservation of a competitive edge depend on the organization's separation from the competitive landscape and the presence of protective barriers that safeguard against incursions by rival firms. This isolation process is driven by the distinctiveness and irreproducibility of the organization's history, rendering it unique, unmatched, and hard to replicate, while ensuring that it remains unchanged.

Different factors encourage researchers to reexamine resource-based theory to uncover its untapped potential (Conner, 1991; Conner & Prahalad, 1996). The aim is to establish an analytical framework that explores the process of identifying competitive advantage and highlights how the development of unique skills is an ongoing phenomenon that evolves progressively over time. To address the constraints identified by resource-based theory, a novel strategy has been suggested that emphasizes the importance of dynamic capabilities. Specifically, the innovative method emphasizes that merely having skills is insufficient for organizations; it is essential that these skills are unique and distinctive, i.e., not held by other organizations, and allow the organization to differentiate itself from competitors (Valaei et al., 2022).

As a result, based on the *dynamic capability model* (Zahra et al., 2006; Bitencourt et al., 2020; Wang & Ahmed, 2007), establishing a competitive edge is not merely about accumulating a stock of resources. Instead, it primarily relies on the capacity to exchange, utilize, combine, adapt, and rejuvenate those resources over time, keeping as it is. Numerous benefits arise from the latter approach: to ensure sustainability and maintain a competitive edge in a rapidly changing environment, it is crucial to concentrate on dynamic capabilities, which refer to the ongoing enhancement of value creation abilities. Consequently, the dynamic capabilities approach emphasizes how businesses renew their competencies in a volatile setting. It is common for organizations with the same goals and fundamental abilities to have varying levels of performance. This imbalance can be attributed not primarily to the organization's skill in choosing, gathering, and utilizing resources but more to its capability to combine and utilize them collaboratively. Dynamic capabilities are thus recognized as the capacity to adjust, combine, and reorganize both internal and external organizational processes. By recombining essential skills, dynamic capabilities create competencies that enable enterprises to seize opportunities. Opening skills focus on facilitating the revitalization, enhancement, and restoration of fundamental abilities.

The connection between dynamic capabilities and opening skills can be characterized as a cyclical one, where dynamic capabilities influence opening skills through their integration and reintegration, thereby promoting the revitalization of the organization's competencies.

Therefore, if the *resource-based theory* approach emphasizes the static dimension of knowledge, not capturing the ways in which the organization's distinctive skills are sedimented, the new approach instead focuses on the dynamic dimension of knowledge, emphasizing the functioning of the processes according to which knowledge and skills are sedimented in the organization.

2.6 Dynamism and Circularity of Knowledge

Organization is unable to generate knowledge independently. The organization needs to share individual insights to enhance collective knowledge. This requires some time. The development of organizational knowledge is thus a cyclical process that begins at the individual level and advances through interactions among various departments and divisions and ultimately encompasses the whole organization (Bratianu et al., 2011).

In a time characterized by swift technological and social transformations, the speed economy is crucial: an organization lacking the essential expertise is unlikely to withstand fierce global competition. Valuable tacit knowledge serves as a foundation for a lasting competitive edge, as it requires significant time to develop and cannot be easily copied. Simultaneously, the organization must convert its implicit knowledge into explicit knowledge and implement it efficiently and promptly to maintain its competitiveness in the market.

Dynamism of knowledge requires the satisfaction of several assumptions that must occur within an organization (Spender, 1996):

1. *Minimum variety required*. The organization that intends to face environmental challenges must harmonize its internal diversity with internal variety and complexity. Organizational members can respond to changing contexts only by combining information more flexibly and quickly and by giving every part of the organization the same access possibilities, reducing the number of steps to a minimum.
2. *Organizational intentionality* understood as the organization's aspiration to achieve its objectives. Organizational intentionality constitutes the prerequisite for evaluating the veracity of knowledge. Without intentionality, it is difficult to establish the value of information or knowledge perceived or created.
3. *Minimum variety required*. The organization that intends to face environmental challenges must harmonize its internal diversity with internal variety and complexity. Organizational members can respond to changing contexts only by combining information more flexibly and quickly and by giving every part of the organization the same access possibilities, reducing the number of steps to a minimum.
4. *Autonomy*. The organization that favors the autonomous action of its members can increase the chances of generating unexpected opportunities and original ideas that spread throughout the group and thus become organizational knowledge. Autonomy also increases the likelihood that individuals will be motivated to create new knowledge.
5. *Redundancy*. Sharing redundant information allows people to understand their place within the organization to control the direction of individual thought and action and represents a self-control mechanism for the organization that allows it to maintain the set course.
6. *Creative chaos*. The presence of fluctuations breaks the habits of organizational members and causes disruptions in habitual ways of thinking. These occurrences

encourage individuals to rethink their thoughts and typical behaviors by promoting a profound engagement, as they enhance the interaction between the organization and its external environment. The ongoing examination and reevaluation of assumptions by each member of the organization contributes to the development of organizational knowledge.

Organization generates new insights by reconciling the various conflicts it consistently encounters while interacting with the external environment. These inconsistencies ultimately impact how organizational boundaries are defined.

2.7 Repatriate Knowledge Transfer in Organizations

Transfer of knowledge is becoming a crucial factor for organizations seeking to achieve a competitive edge and differentiate themselves from competitors. Repatriation serves as a crucial asset for this procedure. People who take on international assignments overseas acquire valuable experiences and knowledge that can greatly benefit organizations (Reis et al., 2024).

Repatriates can significantly contribute to the organization's global social network, as they can facilitate the quick exchange of knowledge between subsidiaries and affiliates and the parent organization, and vice versa (Jayasingam et al., 2021). Additionally, the repatriation procedure is a significant area of research, as an employee's tenure within an organization is influenced by how effectively the repatriation process is carried out (Knocke & Schuster, 2017). Additionally, repatriation challenges tend to be more complex, less obvious, and frequently underestimated in comparison to the difficulties faced during expatriation. The transfer of knowledge by the repatriate not only aids in the development and generation of new information for the organization but also provides a foundation for suggesting enhancements to present organizational procedures (Reiche, 2012; Chiang et al., 2018).

In addition, organizations enhance their chances of achieving success in global expansion by generating and sharing knowledge internally, which also facilitates quicker adaptation to evolving circumstances (Vidal et al., 2007). It is essential to recognize that repatriates, through their experiences in diverse geographical areas, gather knowledge that can prove beneficial to the parent organization, as it offers valuable perspectives on different facets of international markets. All these elements play a role in enhancing the organization's competitive edge (Nery-Kjerfve & McLean, 2012).

The processes of knowledge transfer and absorption are fluid and constantly evolving. During their time at the host organization, repatriates create networks and develop social capital, allowing them to gain access to knowledge and information (Mäkelä & Brewster, 2009; Reiche, 2012). As a result, they might still remain informed about advancements in the host organization, which could influence their actions within the home organization. Furthermore, when repatriates perceive support from their organization, they are more inclined to apply the knowledge they have recently acquired.

On the other hand, if returning expatriates do not experience this support, they are more inclined to depart from the multinational corporation, which may lead to the knowledge they have previously acquired becoming irrelevant and outdated for the organization. Nonetheless, the lasting impacts of repatriates on the organization and the length of time they serve as channels of knowledge have not been thoroughly examined (Chiang et al., 2018).

When repatriates feel appreciated and acknowledged by the headquarters, they are more inclined to maintain relationships with the host organizations, which will lead to a more enduring competitive edge over time.

How Can Organizations Encourage Repatriates to Share Their Knowledge?

The process of knowledge transfer from repatriates can be affected by various elements, one of which is how well the repatriate adjusts back into the parent organization. Typically, repatriates who are welcomed positively upon their return demonstrate a readiness to share the insights gained during their time abroad. On the other hand, certain repatriates face challenges during their reintegration stemming from reverse culture shock (Chiang et al., 2018; Peltokorpi et al., 2022; Shao et al., 2022).

Upon departing from their native country, expatriates must adjust to the customs and norms of different countries and institutions. Upon their return as repatriates, individuals face comparable circumstances and frequently encounter difficulties in acclimating to the culture of their home country and the organization itself (Hao & Liu, 2017). This reverse cultural shock is especially strong for workers coming from culturally uniform backgrounds, as they have experienced significant changes while overseas and must make considerable adjustments to their former habits (Nery-Kjerfve & McLean, 2012). Moreover, inadequate reintegration may occur when organizations do not provide repatriates with roles that align with the skills and experiences they gained while abroad, which can result in decreased motivation among those returning (Vidal et al., 2007).

These elements may lead repatriates to experience dissatisfaction with their jobs, which can ultimately result in them departing from the organization without sharing the knowledge they acquired while abroad (Chiang et al., 2018; Nery-Kjerfve & McLean, 2012).

Furthermore, certain traits of repatriates, including cultural awareness, skills in establishing relationships, and prior experiences as expatriates, may affect the process of knowledge transfer (Oleškevičiūtė et al., 2022). The expectations of repatriates may additionally act as a potential precursor to the results of the repatriation process (Chiang et al., 2018). In numerous instances, repatriates tend to have expectations that surpass what the organization anticipated for them, which frequently results in disappointment, especially regarding their career advancement (Peltonen, 1997).

Therefore, it is essential for multinational organizations to support repatriates in establishing realistic expectations throughout their time abroad and upon their return home (Chiang et al., 2018).

One could contend that support from the organization is crucial throughout the processes of expatriation and repatriation. When expatriates receive support from their supervisors while abroad, their re-entry into their home country is more likely to be seamless, thanks to the development of trust-based relationships (Valk et al., 2013).

Managers must thoughtfully develop and assess approaches that focus on retaining expatriates. Creating policies focused on human resources support is essential for facilitating the adaptation of repatriates (Howe-Walsh & Torka, 2017). Additionally, it is advisable to distinctly separate repatriates from regular employees, depending on the circumstances surrounding the repatriates (Shao et al., 2022; Stevens et al., 2006).

Transfer of knowledge from repatriates can play a crucial role for organizations. Employees from the home country gain an enhanced comprehension of international business practices, cultures, and markets, providing multinationals with a valuable strategic asset that is hard for rivals to replicate (Bucher et al., 2022; Crowne, 2009).

In the context of international assignments, expatriates are responsible for disseminating knowledge from the headquarters to overseas subsidiaries (Edström & Galbraith, 1977; Froese et al., 2021).

Simultaneously, throughout this process, expatriates gain various forms of knowledge that are valuable to the parent organization, including insights specific to the market, personal competencies, management abilities related to their work, networking capabilities, and overall management skills (Fink & Meierewert, 2005).

Through the first option, expatriates gain fresh insights into the business landscape of the foreign nation as well as the cultural distinctions between their home country and the host country. Personal skills pertain to a person's character and can often align with traits such as self-confidence, adaptability, and open-mindedness. Conversely, work-related abilities emphasize the technical expertise and professional skills that repatriates are required to share with their peers (Vidal et al., 2007). Networking abilities are crucial as expatriates build enduring connections with global contacts during their overseas assignments, which can greatly benefit the organization (Oddou et al., 2013; Vidal et al., 2007).

Ultimately, general management abilities enable repatriates to better comprehend the global business framework of the organization. The wealth of knowledge serves as an important resource not just for organizations but also for the employees who undergo considerable personal development.

This expansion can serve as a catalyst for repatriates to enhance their skills and competencies in sharing the knowledge they have gained. For this knowledge to be effectively utilized, it is essential that the skills and expertise of repatriates align with the job requirements at the parent organization. Moreover, the more frequently expatriates communicate with the parent organization throughout the expatriation process, the simpler it becomes for them to share their knowledge upon repatriation

(Froese et al., 2021). Aligned with this idea, it is essential to emphasize that successful knowledge transfer necessitates a suitable match between the repatriate's motivation to share their insights and the organization's readiness to embrace that information (Lazarova & Tarique, 2005).

Repatriates ought to have valuable knowledge for the organization and show both the willingness and eagerness to share their experiences.

This drive may stem from the repatriate's evaluation of the costs and advantages associated with this process, leading them to make decisions influenced by anticipated rewards such as enhanced influence, esteem, recognition, and the opportunity costs related to the time and effort invested. Conversely, organizations need to possess the appropriate tools to capture knowledge and establish the right incentives for returning employees to embrace this process (Gonzalez & Chakraborty, 2014).

Amir et al. (2020) recommend several actions that organizations ought to take to achieve favorable outcomes in knowledge transfer from repatriates. One important aspect is to focus not just on expatriation but also on repatriation, as previously highlighted, ensuring that the international assignment yields positive outcomes for both the repatriate and the organization. To put it differently, the processes of expatriation and repatriation ought to be viewed as a cohesive cycle that includes three stages: prior to expatriation, throughout expatriation, and following repatriation (Burmeister & Deller, 2016).

In addition to this, it is important to conduct frequent debriefings throughout the expatriation process. This will ensure that expatriates are aware of any changes occurring within the parent organization and are not caught off guard when it comes time for repatriation.

It is important to recognize that repatriates often take the lead in sharing their knowledge, rather than other staff actively looking for this information. The readiness of repatriates can be attributed to four factors: having the appropriate knowledge, being at the right time, maintaining the right attitude, and being in the right work environment (Oddou et al., 2013). This indicates that repatriates need to demonstrate how their expertise connects to the challenges the organization is addressing, ensuring that employees grasp the background of the information being provided to them. Additionally, it is crucial for the repatriate to apply their knowledge at the right moment, considering the circumstances of the organization. During this phase of knowledge exchange, it is essential for repatriates to exhibit the appropriate mindset, which includes traits like patience, determination, and an aptitude for inspiring others. Ultimately, it is crucial to highlight that the entire process becomes simpler when the repatriate is in an optimal situation to utilize their skills effectively.

Organizations have the capacity to facilitate the sharing and internalization of repatriates' knowledge by utilizing human resources strategies that include training and communication methods (Shao et al., 2022). Nonetheless, it is essential to understand that knowledge transfer functions as an educational process shaped by both the repatriate, who possesses the information and must be capable of effectively communicating it, and the employees, who are the recipients and must be able to comprehend and integrate the information (Burmeister et al., 2018).

Leaders significantly contribute to the process of knowledge absorption by serving as intermediaries between repatriates and employees, creating an atmosphere that supports the transfer of knowledge (Bucher et al., 2022).

Repatriates recognize that they have gained valuable insights and established a global network during their assignments, experiences that they would not have obtained if they had remained at the organization's headquarters.

Upon their return to the home organization, individuals anticipate advancement in their careers, both in tangible ways, such as promotions and salary hikes, and in more personal terms, through the fulfillment of organization objectives, especially regarding acknowledgment for the expertise and abilities gained during their time abroad (Chiang et al., 2018). Upon their return to their original organizations, repatriates might encounter roles that do not leverage their skills and experience to the fullest, frequently because of inadequate career planning after repatriation.

This disparity may result in lower performance levels and a feeling of diminished loyalty to the organization (Gonzalez & Chakraborty, 2014). They might also be assigned to positions that do not correspond with or utilize the experience acquired at the host organization (Cave et al., 2022; Nery-Kjerfve & McLean, 2012). It is important to acknowledge that repatriates might also be placed in different departments that align more with their expertise or even take on new international roles, which could lessen their intentions to leave the organization.

2.8 Knowledge Generation to Enhancing Creativity

The idea of knowledge is intimately connected to the notion of creativity. Creativity has been examined from multiple perspectives, yet only a handful of theories have provided a compelling rationale: it remains one of the most challenging cognitive processes to comprehend and articulate (Shahzad et al., 2016; Bettiol et al., 2012; Sigala & Chalkiti, 2015).

Certain writers view creativity as a cognitive skill that encompasses the capacity to recognize issues (problem identification) and to develop solutions (solution generation and problem-solving) by employing both divergent and convergent thinking methods. Creativity is seen to highlight the connection between creativity and knowledge. In this perspective, technical, managerial, and market expertise, along with individual abilities, are crucial to the creative process.

A significant portion of the theory describes creativity as a system's ability to undergo evolution. Creativity is not merely a trivial trait of an individual; rather, it is an optimistic mindset aimed at transformation, evolution, and innovation. The aim of creativity extends beyond just humans; it encompasses any system that can undergo transformation.

Nonetheless, while change is essential, it alone does not fully capture the essence of creativity. Indeed, the system needs to possess the capability to develop over time. In general, a system is considered creative when it can evolve in a manner that is not predetermined or known in advance, making it impossible to define beforehand.

In recent years, studies on creativity have increased in the managerial field. The approach most followed by experts is called *de-compositionist* (Vicari & Troilo, 2000). It allows us to understand the conditions that must exist for individuals to unleash their creative potential, organizational levers that must be adopted to stimulate individuals to think creatively (overcoming the cognitive patterns of the past and internalizing new points of view), and the techniques that individuals must implement to free themselves from the ways of interpreting reality.

Creativity does not imply having original ideas; it is an organization's ability to modify reality, i.e., the environment in which the organization operates. Creativity can be characterized as a cyclical process in which a creative organization not only needs to produce fresh, original concepts but also must effectively convert these ideas into actions that can result in innovation. The sole alteration of cognitive frameworks that does not lead to uncreative actions or changes is a unique idea that fails to generate any substantial economic impact: it is merely a trivial adjustment (Botega & da Silva, 2020).

Creative organization needs to possess the capacity to adapt, adjust its behavior, and change its approach. This capability needs to be associated with the proficiency in creating a new reference framework, a different environment, or a new scenario that distinguishes itself from the earlier ones. Any imaginative system can alter reality, impact the surrounding environment, change its relations to the context, and influence other subjects.

The innovative firm has the capability to establish new frameworks, understands how to invigorate a fresh market, introduces new offerings, has the power to adapt its processes, and can foster agreement regarding its operations among clients, suppliers, investors, and financial backers.

Creative organizations cultivate their ability to evolve by responding to the disruptions from their surrounding environment, beginning with the challenges they encounter.

The innovative organization responds to business challenges by discovering fresh ideas, novel solutions, new products, and different strategies for entering the market. Disruptions encourage the organization to enhance its innovative abilities.

For all organizations, challenges serve as significant opportunities for expansion since they frequently unleash energy that enables them to confront crises and create a momentum strong enough to trigger processes that yield meaningful outcomes. This happens through (1) the management's capability to enhance overall environmental disturbances within the organization and establish highly ambitious goals and (2) utilizing crisis scenarios to stimulate the organization's creative potential.

Organizations leverage disruption, and by harnessing their creativity, they can enhance both success and profitability.

Moments of crisis, i.e., when the organization moves away from the point of equilibrium, are fundamental for the survival of the organization because its ability to evolve depends on the difficulty and its ability to generate creativity in the face of disturbances.

In this era of complexity, the advancement of research on cognitive dynamics stands out as one of the major challenges facing business disciplines. On the one hand, environmental instability leads to a persistent disqualification of existing knowledge and a rising necessity to enhance cognitive demands by restructuring that knowledge; on the other hand, learning, i.e., the ability to generate new knowledge, fuels the dynamism of competitive contexts.

In highly competitive environments, the likelihood of survival relies on the intense flow of information both within and outside the organization. They enable you to modify your actions and respond to emerging opportunities. Therefore, the essential function of knowledge and the capacity to create new knowledge becomes apparent: learning transforms into the approach that the organization needs to adopt to navigate environmental diversity and fluctuations, thereby achieving a strong position to manage complexity effectively (Alzghoul et al., 2018).

In the subsequent paragraphs, we will explore how a learning-focused organization will not only generate new insights about the complexities it faces but will primarily focus on facilitating collaboration among its members. This transformation aims to shift knowledge from being an individual resource to becoming a collective organizational asset.

References

Ackoff, R. L. (1989). From data to wisdom. *Journal of Applied Systems Analysis, 16*, 3–9.

Akpur, U. (2024). Does creativity matter in personality traits and emotional intelligence? *Psychology in the Schools, 61*, 3612–3625. https://doi.org/10.1002/pits.23245

Alhadeff-Jones, M. (2008). Three generations of complexity theories: Nuances and ambiguities. *Educational Philosophy and Theory, 40*(1), 66–82. https://doi.org/10.1111/j.1469-5812.2007.00411.x

Allen, G. D. (2017). Hierarchy of knowledge—from data to wisdom. *International Journal of Current Research in Multidisciplinary, 2*, 15–23.

Alvarez, S. A., & Barney, J. B. (2000). Entrepreneurial capabilities: A resource-based view. In G. D. Meyer & K. A. Heppard (Eds.), *Entrepreneurship as strategy: Competing on the entrepreneurial edge* (pp. 63–82). Sage.

Alzghoul, A., Elrehail, H., Emeagwali, O. L., & AlShboul, M. K. (2018). Knowledge management, workplace climate, creativity and performance: The role of authentic leadership. *Journal of Workplace Learning, 30*(8), 592–612. https://doi.org/10.1108/JWL-12-2017-0111

Amir, S., Okimoto, T. G., & Moeller, M. (2020). Informal repatriate knowledge transfer: A qualitative analysis of Malaysian corporate executives. *Journal of Global Mobility, 8*(1), 107–140. https://doi.org/10.1108/JGM-09-2019-0043

Argyris, C. (1977). Double loop learning in organizations. *Harvard Business Review, 55*(5), 115–125.

Argyris, C. (1999). *On organizational learning*. Oxford University Press.

Argyris, C., & Schon, D. (1978). *Organizational learning: A theory of action perspective*. Addison-Wesley.

Bar-Hillel, Y., & Carnap, R. (1953). Semantic Information. *British Journal for the Philosophy of Science., 4*, 147–157.

Barnard, C. (1938). *The functions of the executive*. Harvard University Press.

Barney, J. B. (1986). Strategic factor markets: Expectations, luck and business strategy. *Management Science, 42*, 1231–1241.

Barney, J. B. (1991). Firm resources and sustained competitive advantage. *Journal of Management, 17*, 99–120.

Barney, J. B. (2001). Is the resource-based view a useful perspective for strategic management research? Yes. *Academy of Management Review, 26*, 41–56.

Bettiol, M., Di Maria, E., & Grandinetti, R. (2012). Codification and creativity: knowledge management strategies in KIBS. *Journal of Knowledge Management, 16*(4), 550–562. https://doi.org/10.1108/13673271211246130

Bitencourt, C. C., De Oliveira Santini, F., Ladeira, W. J., Santos, A. C., & Kunzel Teixeira, E. (2020). The extended dynamic capabilities model: A meta-analysis. *European Management Journal, 38*(1), 108–120. https://doi.org/10.1016/j.emj.2019.04.007

Botega, L. F. D. C., & da Silva, J. C. (2020). An artificial intelligence approach to support knowledge management on the selection of creativity and innovation techniques. *Journal of Knowledge Management, 24*(5), 1107–1130. https://doi.org/10.1108/JKM-10-2019-0559

Bratianu, C., & Leon, R. D. (2015). Strategies to enhance intergenerational learning and reducing knowledge loss: An empirical study of universities. *VINE Journal of Information and Knowledge Management Systems, 45*, 551–567.

Bratianu, C., Agapie, A., Orzea, I., & Agoston, S. (2011). Inter-generational learning dynamics in universities. *Electronic Journal of Knowledge Management, 9*(1), 10–18.

Bratianu, C., & Bejinaru, R. (2023). From knowledge to wisdom: Looking beyond the knowledge hierarchy. *Knowledge, 3*, 196–214. https://doi.org/10.3390/knowledge3020014

Bratianu, C., Prelipcean, G., & Bejinaru, R. (2020). Exploring the latent variables, which support SMEs to become learning organizations. *Management & Marketing. Challenges for the Knowledge Society, 15*(2), 154–171.

Bratianu, C., Vatamanescu, E. M., Anagnoste, S., & Gandolfo, D. (2021). Untangling knowledge fields and knowledge dynamics within the decision-making process. *Management Decision, 59*, 306–323.

Bucher, J., Burmeister, A., Osland, J. S., & Deller, J. (2022). The influence of empowering leadership on repatriate knowledge transfer: Understanding mechanisms and boundary conditions. *International Journal of Human Resource Management, 33*(7), 1437–1462. https://doi.org/10.1080/09585192.2020.1771400

Burmeister, A., & Deller, J. (2016). A practical perspective on repatriate knowledge transfer: The influence of organizational support practices. *Journal of Global Mobility, 4*(1), 68–87. https://doi.org/10.1108/JGM-09-2015-0041

Burmeister, A., Lazarova, M. B., & Deller, J. (2018). Repatriate knowledge transfer: Antecedents and boundary conditions of a dyadic process. *Journal of World Business, 53*(6), 806–816. https://doi.org/10.1016/j.jwb.2018.06.004

Cave, A. H., Roberts, M. J., & Muralidharan, E. (2022). Examining antecedents of repatriates' job engagement and its influence on turnover intention. *The International Journal of Human Resource Management*, 1–34. https://doi.org/10.1080/09585192.2022.2145911

Chiang, F. F. T., van Esch, E., Birtch, T. A., & Shaffer, M. A. (2018). Repatriation: what do we know and where do we go from here. *International Journal of Human Resource Management, 29*(1), 188–226. https://doi.org/10.1080/09585192.2017.1380065

Choo, C. W. (2006). *The knowing organization: How organizations use information to construct meaning, create knowledge, and make decisions* (2nd ed.). Oxford University Press.

Connelly, C. E., Zweig, D., Webster, J., & Trougakos, J. P. (2012). Knowledge hiding in organizations. *Journal of Organizational Behaviour, 33*, 64–88.

Conner, K. R. (1991). An historical comparison of resource-based theory and five schools of thought within industrial organization economics: Do we have a new theory of the firm? *Journal of Management, 17*, 121–154.

Conner, K. R., & Prahalad, C. K. (1996). A resource-based theory of the firm: Knowledge versus opportunism. *Organization Science, 7*(5), 477–501.

Crowne, K. A. (2009). Enhancing knowledge transfer during and after international assignments. *Journal of Knowledge Management, 13*(4), 134–147. https://doi.org/10.1108/13673270910971888

Damasio, A. (2012). *Self comes to mind: Constructing the conscious brain*. Vintage Books.

Dar-EI, E. (2000). *Human learning: From learning curves to learning organizations*. Springer.

Davenport, T. H., & Prusak, L. (2000). *Working knowledge: How organizations manage what they know*. Harvard Business School Press.

Dollinger, S. J., Palaskonis, D. G., & Pearson, J. L. (2004). Creativity and intuition revisited. *The Journal of Creative Behavior, 38*, 244–259. https://doi.org/10.1002/j.2162-6057.2004.tb01243.x

Dooley, K. (2002). In M. Warner (Ed.), *Organizational complexity, international encyclopedia of business and management* (pp. 5013–5022). Thompson Learning.

Edström, A., & Galbraith, J. R. (1977). Transfer of managers as a coordination and control strategy in multinational organizations. *Administrative Science Quarterly, 22*(2), 248–263. https://doi.org/10.2307/2391959

Fink, G., & Meierewert, S. (2005). The use of repatriate knowledge in organizations. *Human Resource Planning, 28*(4), 30–36.

Froese, F. J., Stoermer, S., Reiche, B. S., & Klar, S. (2021). Best of both worlds: How embeddedness fit in the host unit and the headquarters improve repatriate knowledge transfer. *Journal of International Business Studies, 52*(7), 1331–1349. https://doi.org/10.1057/s41267-020-00356-4

Gladwell, M. (2005). *Blink: The power of thinking without thinking*. Back Bay Books.

Glock, C. H., Grosse, E. H., Jaber, M. Y., & Smunt, T. L. (2019). Applications of learning curves in production and operations management: A systematic literature review. *Computers & Industrial Engineering, 131*, 422–441. https://doi.org/10.1016/j.cie.2018.10.030

Gonzalez, J. A., & Chakraborty, S. (2014). Expatriate knowledge utilization and MNE performance: A multilevel framework. *Human Resource Management Review, 24*(4), 299–312. https://doi.org/10.1016/j.hrmr.2014.03.001

Grant, R. M., & Baden-Fuller, C. (1995). A knowledge-based theory of inter-firm collaboration. Academy of Management, Best Papers Proceedings, (pp. 17–21).

Hall, S. S. (2010). *Wisdom: From philosophy to neuroscience*. Alfred A. Knopf.

Hao, J., & Liu, Q. (2017). The impact of Australian accounting education on repatriates' career development. *Australian Accounting Review, 27*(1), 52–60. https://doi.org/10.1111/auar.12141

Hladchenko, M. (2016). Knowledge valorisation: A route of knowledge that ends in surplus value (an example of The Netherlands). *International Journal of Educational Management, 30*(5), 668–678. https://doi.org/10.1108/IJEM-12-2014-0167

Holden, N., & Glisby, M. (2010). *Creating knowledge advantage: The Tacit dimension of international competition and cooperation*. Copenhagen Business School Press.

Horn, J. (2008). Human research and complexity theory. *Educational Philosophy and Theory, 40*(1), 130–143. https://doi.org/10.1111/j.1469-5812.2007.00395.x

Howe-Walsh, L., & Torka, N. (2017). Repatriation and (perceived) organisational support (POS): The role of and interaction between repatriation supporters. *Journal of Global Mobility, 5*(1), 60–77. https://doi.org/10.1108/JGM-09-2016-0040

Iván Tarride, M. (2013). The complexity of measuring complexity. *Kybernetes, 42*(2), 174–184. https://doi.org/10.1108/03684921311310558

Jashapara, A. (2011). *Knowledge management: An integrated approach* (2nd ed.). Financial Times/Prentice Hall.

Jayasingam, S., Chong, M. M., & Abu Bakar, R. (2021). Knowledge sharing behaviour of overqualified repatriates. *Journal of Global Mobility, 9*(4), 543–573. https://doi.org/10.1108/JGM-04-2021-0050

Jung, C. G. (1929). Problems of modern psychotherapy, Coll. Wks, 16.

Kahneman, D. (2011). *Thinking, fast and slow*. Farrar, Straus and Giroux.

Klir, G. J. (1985). Complexity: Some general observations. *Systems Research, 2*(2), 131–140. https://doi.org/10.1002/sres.3850020205

Knocke, J., & Schuster, T. (2017). Repatriation of international assignees: Where are we and where do we go from here? A systematic literature review. *Journal of Global Mobility, 5*(3), 275–303. https://doi.org/10.1108/JGM-01-2017-0001

Kogut, B., & Zander, U. (1992). Knowledge of the firm, combinative capabilities, and the replication of technology. *Organization Science, 3*, 383–397.

Kolb, D. A. (2015). *Experiential learning: Experience as the source of learning and development* (2nd ed.). Pearson Education.

Lane, P., & Lubatkin, M. (1998). Relative absorptive capacity and interorganizational learning. *Strategic Management Journal, 19*, 461–477.

Lazarova, M., & Tarique, I. (2005). Knowledge transfer upon repatriation. *Journal of World Business, 40*(4), 361–373. https://doi.org/10.1016/j.jwb.2005.08.004

Lebel, L., & Lorek, S. (2009). Production–consumption systems and the pursuit of sustainability. In L. Lebel, S. Lorek, & R. Daniel (Eds.), *Sustainable production consumption systems*. Springer. https://doi.org/10.1007/978-90-481-3090-0_1

Liebowitz, J. (1997). Knowledge-based/expert systems technology in life support systems. *Kybernetes, 26*(5), 555–573.

Liebowitz, J. (2000). *Building organizational intelligence: A knowledge management primer*. CRC Press.

Liew, A. (2013). DIKIW: Data, information, knowledge, intelligence, wisdom and their Interrelationships. *Business Management Dynamics, 2*, 49–62.

Mäkelä, K., & Brewster, C. (2009). Interunit interaction contexts, interpersonal social capital, and the differing levels of knowledge sharing. *Human Resource Management, 45*(1), 127–145. https://doi.org/10.1002/hrm

Manson, S. M. (2001). Simplifying complexity: A review of complexity theory. *Geoforum, 32*(3), 405–414. https://doi.org/10.1016/S0016-7185(00)00035-X

Mayo, E. (1945). *The social problems of an industrial civilization*. Division of Research, Harvard Business School.

McAfee, A., & Brynjolfsson, E. (2012). Big data: The management revolution. *Harvard Business Review, 90*, 60–68.

Metaxiotis, K., Ergazakis, K., Samouilidis, E., & Psarras, J. (2003). Decision support through knowledge management: The role of the artificial intelligence. *Information Management & Computer Security, 11*(5), 216–221.

Moldoveanu, M. C., & Bauer, R. M. (2004). On the relationship between organizational complexity and organizational structuration. *Organization Science, 15*(1), 98–118. https://doi.org/10.1287/orsc.1030.0058

Narvekar, R. S., & Jain, K. (2006). A new framework to understand the technological innovation process. *Journal of Intellectual Capital, 7*(2), 174–186. https://doi.org/10.1108/14691930610661845

Nelson, R., & Winter, S. (1982). *An evolutionary theory of economic change*. Harvard University Press.

Nery-Kjerfve, T., & McLean, G. N. (2012). Repatriation of expatriate employees, knowledge transfer, and organizational learning: What do we know? *European Journal of Training and Development, 36*(6), 614–629. https://doi.org/10.1108/03090591211245512

Nieto, M. (2004). Basic propositions for the study of the technological innovation process in the firm. *European Journal of Innovation Management, 7*(4), 314–324. https://doi.org/10.1108/14601060410565065

Nonaka, I., & Takeuchi, H. (2019). *The wise company: How companies create continuous innovation*. Oxford University Press.

Nonaka, I., & Takeuchi, H. (1995). *The knowledge-creating company: How Japanese companies create the dynamics of innovation*. Oxford University Press.

Oddou, G., Szkudlarek, B., Osland, J. S., Deller, J., Blakeney, R., & Furuya, N. (2013). Organizational dynamics repatriates as a source of competitive advantage. How to manage knowledge transfer. *Organizational Dynamics, 42*(4), 257–266. https://doi.org/10.1016/j.orgdyn.2013.07.003

Oleškevičiūtė, E., Dickmann, M., Andresen, M., & Parry, E. (2022). The international transfer of individual career capital: Exploring and developing a model of the underlying factors. *Journal of Global Mobility*, 765355. https://doi.org/10.1108/JGM-12-2020-0082

Pappas, G. F. (2016). John Dewey's radical logic: The function of the qualitative in thinking. *Transactions of the Charles S. Peirce Society, 52*(3), 435–468. https://doi.org/10.2979/trancharpeirsoc.52.3.08

Peltokorpi, V., Froese, F. J., Reiche, B. S., & Klar, S. (2022). Reverse knowledge flows: How and when do preparation and reintegration facilitate repatriate knowledge transfer? *Journal of Management Studies*. https://doi.org/10.1111/joms.12802

Peltonen, T. (1997). Facing the rankings from the past: A tournament perspective on repatriate career mobility. *International Journal of Human Resource Management, 8*(1), 106–123. https://doi.org/10.1080/095851997000000043

Penrose, E. T. (1959). *The theory of the growth of the firm*. Wiley.

Peteraf, M. (1993). The cornerstones of competitive advantage: A resource-based view. *Strategic Management Journal, 13*, 363–380.

Phelan, S. E. (2001). What is complexity science, really? *Emergence, 3*(1), 120–136. https://doi.org/10.1207/S15327000EM0301_08

Pinker, S. (2008). *The stuff of thought: Language as a window into human nature*. Pinguin Books.

Polanyi. (1958). *Personal knowledge: Towards a post-critical philosophy*. University of Chicago Press.

Polanyi, M. (1983). *The tacit dimension*. Peter Smith.

Primas, H. (2017). *Knowledge and time*. Springer.

Reiche, B. S. (2012). Knowledge benefits of social capital upon repatriation: A longitudinal study of international assignees. *Journal of Management Studies, 49*(6), 1052–1077. https://doi.org/10.1111/j.1467-6486.2012.01050.x

Reis, A. P., Sá, I., Costa, R. M., & Moreira, A. C. (2024). Repatriate's knowledge transfer: Antecedents of knowledge transfer, transfer process, knowledge absorption, and consequences. In M. Valeri (Ed.), *Knowledge management and knowledge sharing. Business strategies and an emerging theoretical field*. Springer.

Richards, O. C., Avery, D. R., Luksyte, A., Boncoeur, O. D., & Spitzmueller, C. (2019). Improving organizational newcomers' creative job performance through creative process engagement: The moderating role of a synergy diversity climate. *Personnel Psychology, 72*(3), 421–444.

Rowley, J. (2007). The wisdom hierarchy: Representations of the DIKW hierarchy. *Journal of Information Science, 33*, 163–180.

Rumelt, R. P. (1984). Towards a strategic theory of the firm. In R. B. Lamb (Ed.), *Competitive strategic management* (pp. 556–570). Prentice Hall.

Rumelt, R. P. (1987). Theory, strategy, and entrepreneurship. In D. Teece (Ed.), *The competitive challenge* (pp. 137–158). Ballinger.

Samier, H. (2018). Intuition and innovation. In H. Samier (Ed.), *Intuition, creativity, innovation*. Wiley. https://doi.org/10.1002/9781119482932.ch6

Seebohm, T. (1992). The preconscious, the unconscious, and the subconscious: A phenomenological explication. *Man and World, 25*, 505–520. https://doi.org/10.1007/BF01252432

Senge, P. (1999). *The fifth discipline: The art and practice of the learning organization*. Random House.

Shahzad, K., Bajwa, S. U., Siddiqi, A. F. I., Ahmid, F., & Raza Sultani, A. (2016). Integrating knowledge management (KM) strategies and processes to enhance organizational creativity and performance: An empirical investigation. *Journal of Modelling in Management, 11*(1), 154–179. https://doi.org/10.1108/JM2-07-2014-0061

Shannon, C. E. (1948). A mathematical theory of communication. *The Bell System Technical Journal, 27*, 379–423.

Shao, J. J., Bayraktar, S., & Al Ariss, A. (2022). Knowledge transfer of Chinese self-initiated repatriates: Exploring the returnee and company perspectives. *Journal of Business Research, 150*, 12–25. https://doi.org/10.1016/j.jbusres.2022.06.002

Sigala, M., & Chalkiti, K. (2015). Knowledge management, social media and employee creativity. *International Journal of Hospitality Management, 45*, 44–58. https://doi.org/10.1016/j.ijhm.2014.11.003

Smiraglia, R. P. (2014). *The elements of knowledge organization*. Springer.

Spender, J. C. (1996). Making knowledge the basis of a dynamic theory of the firm. *Strategic Management Journal, 17*, 45–62. https://doi.org/10.1002/smj.4250171106

Stevens, M. J., Oddou, G., Furuya, N., Bird, A., & Mendenhall, M. (2006). HR factors affecting repatriate job satisfaction and job attachment for Japanese managers. *International Journal of Human Resource Management, 17*(5), 831–841. https://doi.org/10.1080/09585190600640844

Stitzman, L. (2008). At-one-ment, intuition and 'suchness'. *The International Journal of Psychoanalysis, 85*(5), 1137–1155. https://doi.org/10.1516/9QPH-PY63-QG7M-5H90

Valaei, N., Rezaei, S., Bressolles, G., & Dent, M. M. (2022). Indispensable components of creativity, innovation, and FMCG companies' competitive performance: A resource-based view (RBV) of the firm. *Asia-Pacific Journal of Business Administration, 14*(1), 1–26. https://doi.org/10.1108/APJBA-11-2020-0420

Valk, R., van der Velde, M., van Engen, M., & Szkudlarek, B. (2013). International assignment and repatriation experiences of Indian international assignees in The Netherlands. *International Journal of Organizational Analysis, 21*(3), 335–356. https://doi.org/10.1108/IJOA-Jan-2012-0544

Vicari, S., & Troilo, G. (2000). Organizational creativity: A new perspective from cognitive systems theory. In G. von Krogh, I. Nonaka, & T. Nishiguchi (Eds.), *Knowledge creation*. Palgrave Macmillan. https://doi.org/10.1007/978-1-349-62753-0_4

Vidal, M. E., Valle, R. S., & Aragón, M. I. (2007). Antecedents of repatriates' job satisfaction and its influence on turnover intentions: Evidence from Spanish repatriated managers. *Journal of Business Research, 60*(12), 1272–1281. https://doi.org/10.1016/j.jbusres.2007.05.004

Von Hayek, F. A. (1989). The pretence of knowledge. *The American Economic Review, 79*(6), 3–7. https://www.jstor.org/stable/1914347

Wang, C. L., & Ahmed, P. K. (2007). Dynamic capabilities: A review and research agenda. *International Journal of Management Reviews, 9*, 31–51. https://doi.org/10.1111/j.1468-2370.2007.00201.x

Zahra, S. A., Sapienza, H. J., & Davidsson, P. (2006). Entrepreneurship and dynamic capabilities: A review, model and research agenda. *Journal of Management Studies, 43*, 917–955. https://doi.org/10.1111/j.1467-6486.2006.00616.x

Learning and Organizational Strategy 3

3.1 Knowledge and Learning Organization

If the competitive capacity of the organization is based on the knowledge it incorporates, the entire strategic process must place the latter at its center: beyond the mono- or multi-business nature of an organization and the degree of diversification, the creation of knowledge becomes its core business (Loermans, 2002; Sun, 2003; Valeri, 2024). The organization is no longer conceptualized as a portfolio of products or businesses but as a portfolio of skills that must be acquired, developed, and managed (Bolisani & Bratianu, 2018; Foss, 1999; Jasimuddin, 2008; Oluikpe, 2012; Von Krogh et al., 2012).

What Is Meant by Learning?

Learning means developing new knowledge for action, i.e., adapting the individual's behavioral model to that required by environmental, strategic, organizational, and social variations (Newman & Newman, 2015; Zhang & Wang, 2021).

Learning involves both the acquisition of know-how (i.e., the ability to produce actions) and the acquisition of know-why, i.e., the ability to articulate conceptual knowledge of the experience. Learning, in fact, does not end only in the ability to act based on what has been learned from the past, but it ends in the ability to act differently from the past by projecting ourselves into the future (Adler & Heckscher, 2006; Gallupe, 2001; Hedlund, 1994). You truly gain knowledge from your past once you're unable to repeat the same errors.

Knowledge is no longer merely a legacy to be passed on; rather, it is a continuous stream that must be cultivated and managed, representing the core of an organization. The key knowledge lies in the capacity to consistently generate new insights from present skills, rather than simply holding onto them. Learning is designed to

M. Valeri, *Organizations and Knowledge Management*, Knowledge Management and Organizational Learning 16, https://doi.org/10.1007/978-3-031-97954-5_3

be a continuous process; it happens voluntarily and takes place solely when the individual or organization is inclined to acquire new knowledge (Valeri, 2021).

The learning process is divided into three moments: (1) *variation,* (2) *selection*, and (3) *retention* (Lee & Kirlik, 2013):

1. *Variation* serves as the driving force behind innovation. It is at this point that new information is introduced and existing knowledge within the organizational memory is reorganized, leading to fresh insights and the creation of new knowledge. Literature describes information interpretation as the method through which distributed information is understood in one or more common ways. Consequently, organizational learning is enhanced when there are numerous varying interpretations contributed by the organization's members, along with a significant number of organizational units that share and engage with the interpretations developed by other units. The factors that contribute to the creation of a common interpretation using new information are (1) uniformity of the cognitive maps, i.e., the set of beliefs, the mental representation processes possessed a priori by the organizational units, and uniformity of the way in which the information communicated is structured; (2) the richness of the means of communication; (3) information overload, especially if distributed unevenly among the various organizational units, that distracts and prevents a common interpretation; and (4) unlearning and its effects on learning: unlearning is the process through which the individual puts aside the knowledge acquired because it is obsolete and misleading to make room for new behaviors. Unlearning can therefore be defined as a form of learning (Bontis, 1999).
2. *Selection* represents the filter through which experiences are evaluated and meanings are sought in the inexhaustible cognitive world.
3. *Retention* is the mechanism that enables the preservation and sharing of knowledge within the organization by converting it into guidelines, processes, and artifacts. It serves as the means for developing organizational memory. Organizational memory refers to the collection of resources that enable knowledge to be preserved for future utilization. The success of organizational memory relies on how information is understood and shared, the techniques used for documenting data, the strategies employed to retrieve it, and the connections among various elements within the organization.

Organizations are utilizing artificial intelligence to enhance the effectiveness and efficiency of their organizational memory (Kuntz & Matta, 2002). It provides a degree of accessibility and dependability that surpasses human abilities. As a result, digitizing organizational memory enables both information and additional resources to be located more readily than through official standard sources, thereby enhancing the volume of information that can be stored in the computer.

The main way to learn is through experience. Experience drives the creation of new knowledge to tackle environmental complexities. Based on their experiences, a person makes decisions, conducts assessments, chooses among options, and adapts to their surroundings by altering themselves (Van Zolingen et al., 2001).

Even setbacks can serve as valuable lessons. It serves a therapeutic purpose by encouraging organizational dynamism aimed at achieving more profound and disruptive changes in performance relative to rivals while also enhancing the willingness to accept higher levels of risk. In certain situations, failure is deemed essential for bringing about change and facilitating a much deeper level of learning than what is typically experienced.

From a dynamic perspective, there are two distinct forms of learning: (1) single-loop learning (also known as poietic or adaptive learning) and (2) double-loop learning (referred to as praxis or generative learning). *Single-loop* learning is a type of learning linked to the operational framework of an organization, making it a fundamental component of its capabilities (Argyris, 1977, 1999). This type of learning leads to gradual modifications in the previously established combinations of a structure's abilities. *Double-loop* learning refers to the kind of learning that garners significant attention from the governing body of an organization. It enables alterations to the intellectual legacy and the organizational cultural environment, promoting the creation of new knowledge by transforming the existing operational framework.

3.2 Individual and Organizational Learning

What Is the Relationship Between Organizational Learning and Individual Learning?

For an organization to genuinely commit to learning, simply offering access to information is not enough; it is essential that this knowledge evolves into a lasting organizational resource that remains intact even when its present holders depart from the organization (Donate & De Pablo, 2015).

An organization aiming to enhance its knowledge must encourage its members to share their personal insights and expertise. Once knowledge transforms into collective understanding, the organization can overlook individual members (Ardichvili et al., 2003). Consequently, when an organization loses an employee, the impact does not stem from the loss of the organizational knowledge he possessed but rather from the loss of the unique experiences that individual contributed.

Is the Concept of Organizational Learning Merely the Aggregate of the Individual Learning Experiences of Its Members?

Organizational learning transcends the collective knowledge of individuals, enabling the organization to develop values, mental frameworks, and cognitive models that are significantly more advanced than the attitudes and beliefs of its individual members. Corporate action emerges from the interplay among various participants, serving as a result of shared learning and collaboration among decision-making teams. This is a group that advances the process of experimental research (Hecker, 2012).

It is important to emphasize that both organizational and operational structures can fundamentally change over extended periods through gradual and intricate processes that involve numerous reactions.

Organizational structures are in fact characterized both by a tendency toward rigidity, i.e., poor flexibility and adaptability, and by stickiness, i.e., they resist change; as each structure tends to persist over time, each has its own past history. They are made up of human resources who have gained their experience based on experience, accept slow transformations, and require long times to evolve toward new models through the gradual acquisition of experience and organizational knowledge.

Consequently, exhibiting a propensity for rigidity due to the limited interchangeability of the structures and their inadequate adaptability for purposes beyond their original intent, the organizational and operational frameworks restrict the effectiveness of governance. In comparable circumstances, it is important to foster the educational process, as cultivating and sustaining learning-focused behaviors becomes challenging without suitable organizational values and appropriate incentives.

In the context of organizational learning, the individual involved is a group decision-maker who interacts with various topics, each requiring different expertise, and who is active in diverse functional sectors. The emphasis is placed on the exchanges among corporate leaders as they compare their perspectives and assess the outcomes of their actions. This collaborative process helps transcend the cognitive limitations of individual thinking and decision-making, leading to the formation of shared interpretations.

According to Peter Senge (1990), learning organizations are: "...organizations where people continually expand their capacity to create the results, they truly desire, where new and expansive patterns of thinking are nurtured, where collective aspiration is set free, and where people are continually learning to see the whole together" (Senge, 1990, p. 3). The fundamental reasoning behind these organizations is that in times of swift transformation, only those that are adaptable, flexible, and efficient will thrive. To achieve this, it is suggested that organizations should find ways to harness individuals' dedication and ability to learn at every level (Senge, 1990). Although everyone has the ability to learn, the environments they operate in frequently do not support reflection and active participation.

Additionally, individuals might not possess the resources or conceptual frameworks needed to interpret the circumstances they encounter. Organizations that are consistently growing their ability to shape their future need a significant change in mindset among their members.

As Peter Senge suggests, authentic learning connects with the core of what it means to be human. This is relevant for both persons and institutions. Therefore, for a learning organization, mere survival is insufficient (Senge, 1990). The five elements identified by Peter Senge are believed to be coming together to foster innovative learning organizations (Fig. 3.1). They are *systems thinking, personal mastery, mental models, building shared vision, and team learning.*

Fig. 3.1 Five discipline models. *Source*: Senge (1990)

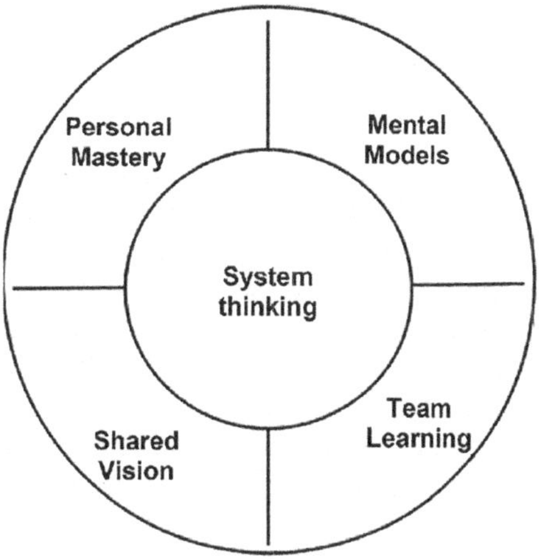

Systems Thinking Systemic thinking is the conceptual cornerstone of his approach. It is the discipline that combines the various disciplines, merging them into a unified framework of theory and application. According to Peter Senge, the strength of systems theory lies in its capacity to understand and tackle the entirety while analyzing the connections among individual components. This capability offers both the motivation and the tools necessary to unify various disciplines.

Personal Mastery It refers to self-realization that breaks through the limits, or skillfulness. The practice involves understanding and enhancing a person's genuine aspirations, focusing attention, fostering patience, and objectively assessing reality. Personal mastery is not something you possess. It is a process. It is a lifelong discipline. Individuals who possess a high degree of personal mastery are deeply conscious of their lack of knowledge, their shortcomings, and the areas in which they can improve. They possess a strong sense of self-confidence. Contradictory? Individuals who have a deep tendency for self-transcendence will consistently pursue knowledge. In traditional hierarchical organizations, the emphasis on promoting self-actualization among employees is frequently neglected. Nevertheless, modern organizations need to focus on the needs of every employee, acknowledging that the employment relationship, individual development, and financial success hold equal importance (Senge, 1990).

Mental Models Discipline of mental models begins with self-reflection; it involves uncovering our internal perceptions of the world, bringing them to light, and examining them critically. It also encompasses the capacity to engage in meaningful dialogues that maintain a balance between questioning and supporting ideas, allowing individuals to clearly express their thoughts while being receptive to the perspectives of others (Senge, 1990). Looking inward is the first step in developing your mental frameworks. Through this process, we discover how to delve into the images of our inner world, bring them to the forefront, and analyze them.

Building Shared Vision If there exists a leadership philosophy that has motivated organizations for millennia, it is the capacity to align with and commit to a common vision. When a true vision exists, individuals thrive and acquire knowledge, not due to external pressure, but out of their own desire to do so. However, numerous leaders possess personal visions that fail to transform into collective visions capable of energizing the organization. The process of cultivating a shared vision encompasses the ability to reveal common *visions of the future* that promote authentic commitment and engagement instead of mere compliance (Senge, 1990). An organization cannot be united without having common goals, values, and missions.

Team Learning The group's collective intelligence surpasses individual knowledge, and the group possesses the overall capability to take action. When a group is truly engaged in learning, it not only achieves outstanding overall outcomes, but its individual members also develop more rapidly compared to other learning approaches. The practice of team learning begins with *dialogue*, which is the ability of team members to set aside their assumptions and engage in true *collective thinking*. *Dialogos* referred to a dynamic exchange of meaning among a group, enabling the collective to uncover insights that individuals alone could not achieve. It also encompasses understanding how to identify the interaction patterns within teams that hinder learning (Senge, 1990). In contemporary organizations, the fundamental unit of learning ought to be the organization itself rather than individual members.

The academic world lacks a clear definition and distinct characteristics of a learning organization. This uncertainty may cause confusion within an organization, leading to the incorrect application of learning organizations in practice. On the other hand, the theory of models regarding learning organizations provides valuable perspectives on organizational learning. Nonetheless, because of its high degree of theoretical abstraction, it stays objectively separated from elements like organizational structure and culture. Therefore, it is essential to conduct a thorough analysis in conjunction with organizational practices.

3.3 Organizational Knowledge Creation

Management literature concurs that a learning organization can be successfully structured and overseen to achieve beneficial outcomes for the organization. Innovation arises solely from the interplay between tacit knowledge and explicit knowledge. The development of organizational knowledge is thus an ongoing and dynamic interplay between tacit and explicit knowledge. This process begins with variations among different modes of knowledge conversion, influenced by multiple triggering factors (Usai et al., 2018; Usman & Musa, 2012; Walczak, 2005).

As of now, there is no universally recognized understanding of what the learning organization's culture should emphasize. Certain academics argue that the foundational strategic elements of a learning organization's culture should include entrepreneurship, risk-taking capabilities, leadership, organizational frameworks, and decentralized strategic planning methods (Allio, 2019; Maheshwari & Yadav, 2019).

Nonaka and Takeuchi (1995) believe that organizational knowledge develops from interactions between tacit knowledge and explicit knowledge (Fig. 3.2).

They focus attention on four ways through which it is possible to ensure that tacit knowledge is put into circulation to increase the organization's knowledge: (1) socialization, (2) externalization, (3) combination, and (4) internalization (SECI model).

Socialization involves the exchange of experiences and the development of implicit knowledge, such as shared mental frameworks and technical abilities. A person can gain tacit knowledge through direct interactions with others, without the need for language to mediate. The key element in acquiring tacit knowledge is practical experience. Without a shared experience, it is difficult for people to imagine themselves in another person's perspective. The straightforward exchange of information may lack significance if it is disconnected from the emotions tied to it and the specific contexts in which the shared experiences originate.

Externalization is the process of expressing tacit knowledge through explicit concepts. It is a process of knowledge creation in which tacit knowledge becomes explicit, taking the form of metaphor, analogy, concept, and hypothesis. Knowledge conversion process in its externalization mode takes place via discussions and shared reflections. In contrast to alternative approaches for transforming knowledge, externalization serves as a crucial strategy for knowledge creation by generating new and explicit ideas from tacit knowledge.

Combination involves organizing concepts into a structured knowledge system. It encompasses the integration of various categories of clear knowledge. People

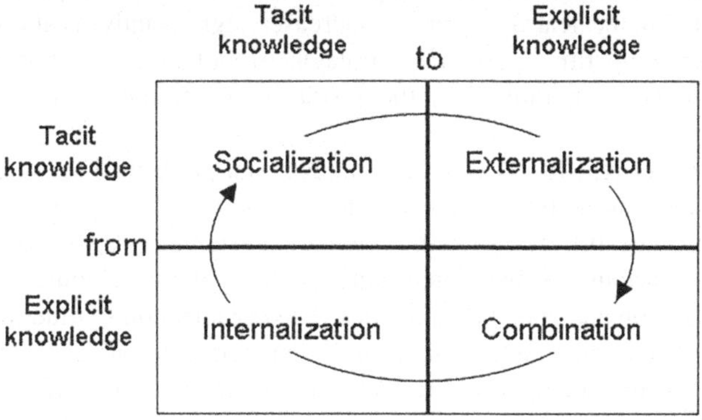

Fig. 3.2 The process of "organizational knowledge creation". Source: Nonaka and Takeuchi (1995)

share and merge knowledge using different methods (such as documents, meetings, and discussions). Reorganizing present information by categorizing, supplementing, and merging explicit knowledge can result in the emergence of new kinds of knowledge.

Internalization consists of concretely translating explicit knowledge and tacit knowledge. Internalization does not always require the actual re-experiencing of other people's experiences; experience in the past can be translated into a tacit mental model. When knowledge is shared by most organizational members, tacit knowledge becomes part of the organizational culture.

The knowledge produced by each of the four conversion methods varies significantly. These pieces of knowledge engage with one another in a dynamic flow referred to by Nonaka and Takeuchi (1995) as the *knowledge spiral*. In the knowledge spiral, both tacit and explicit knowledge grow in quality and quantity through a spiral interaction process that progresses from individuals to groups, and subsequently to organizations, ultimately leading to the generation of new knowledge: *combination* allows the systematization and application of explicit knowledge and information from the group to the organization, *internalization* allows learning and acquiring new tacit knowledge through practice from the organization and then to the individual, *externalization* allows the articulation of tacit knowledge through dialogue and reflection from the individual to the group, and socialization allows the sharing and creation of tacit knowledge between individual and individual, thanks to experience.

3.4 Strategies for Creating a Learning Organization

Does Corporate Strategy Guide Organizational Learning in a Complex Competitive Context?

Many theoretical frameworks have sought to clarify the learning processes that form the basis of organizational development strategies (Argote, 2013; Balle et al., 2020). The approach stems from a learning journey prompted by competitive demands. The intensity of the learning process increases significantly as the organization faces greater competitive pressures. Strategic formulation is a process subject to continuous experimentation, i.e., the result of a constant process of learning by doing.

It is no longer feasible to view the strategy as a predefined set of actions to be executed strictly, as environmental complexity has become more unpredictable, yet it remains manageable. The strategic orientation establishes a shared strategic language across various organizational units, enabling the development of strategies without relying on any specific guidelines. The organization's strategic direction is viewed as the outcome of a learning process that permeates all levels, enabling it to capitalize on available opportunities and meet market demands (King, 2001).

The strategic conduct of an organization is influenced by its strategic focus: the strategic choices made to enhance the organization's potential vary based on the organization's attitudes, goals, style, public image, and expressed values. These factors are a result of its traditions and are deeply ingrained in the individuals who make the decisions.

Mintzberg (1987) identifies three types of strategies: (1) *umbrella strategy* which defines the direction of travel that must be respected by the strategic work of the individual participants in the organization and therefore favors the development of strategic learning; (2) *process strategy* which allows the top management to control only the strategic formulation process and not its content; and (3) *emerging strategy*, i.e., the strategies which are implemented even though they have not been planned a priori by the decision-makers. The process of formulating the three types of strategies presupposes the influence of strategic learning processes.

Normann (2001) focuses his theory on the concept of business idea, defining it as the interface that regulates the relationship between organizations and the environment. Norman defines strategy as a process of adaptive evolution through the processing of information available in a competitive environment.

Despite the relevance of the two different theoretical approaches, Mintzberg and Normann have two different visions regarding the relationship between strategy and learning. According to Mintzberg's analytical perspective, learning operates on the choice between decision alternatives and not on their formation. On the contrary, in Normann's analytical perspective, learning operates in the construction of decision alternatives.

The process of strategic planning entails a rigorous examination by decision-makers, comparing ideas, interpretations, and causal links. This endeavor goes beyond mere negotiation; it is characterized as a cognitive process that offers significant added value. The true aim of successful planning is not merely to create a plan but to transform the mental frameworks of those making decisions (Eisenhardt & Zbaracki, 1992). Acquiring new strategies essentially serves as a catalyst for the strategic reorientation of organizations. This strategic shift is impacted by several factors that should not be overlooked:

1. Heterogeneity of the management team: The greater the heterogeneity, the greater the probability of an effective and efficient redefinition of the strategic orientation.
2. Volatility of the environment: It determines the inadequacy of strategies. This requires a redefinition of strategic behavior.
3. Externalization of failures: This attitude prevents the generation from new strategies.
4. Management turnover rate: Strategic reorientation presupposes the introduction of new managers to develop new interpretations, new visions, and new strategies.

Therefore, the implementation of new strategies requires the presence of new knowledge/skills to support innovative behaviors. This presupposes a cultural change in the organization (Cohen & Levinthal, 1990).

What Is Meant by Strategic Learning and Operational Learning?

In general, we refer to strategic management and operational management, structural choices, and operational choices. Strategic learning constitutes the development of knowledge that attempts, through the proposition of specific knowledge and values, to reduce the complexity of the competitive environment (Boden et al., 2012). By operational learning we mean the set of knowledge aimed at improving the methods of carrying out procedures without changing the basic strategic orientation (Kuwada, 1998; Moon et al., 2017). It is therefore a form of learning that improves the effectiveness and efficiency of knowledge without changing the mental and technological patterns on which the organization's memory is based (Austin, 2003).

Compared to operational learning, strategic learning modifies the cognitive maps that influence strategic decision-making.

Strategic learning operates on three different levels of strategy: (1) *system strategy* (or system architecture), (2) *process strategies* (or meta-strategies), and (3) *structure strategies* (or competitive strategies) (Bood & Postma, 1997):

System strategies concern the definition of the general architecture of the organization. *Process strategies* (or meta-strategies) refer to the selection of the strategy development process and the consequent design of the business system. *Structure strategies* (or competitive strategies) concern the determination of the structural balance of the organization with respect to the markets in which it operates. The organizational strategies define the positioning of the organization in the competitive system. They define the development path that enhances and supports the competitive advantages that the organization possesses and intends to develop.

The connection between strategic learning and operational learning is exemplified by the organization's unique capabilities. These capabilities, alongside the human, technical, and financial resources utilized by the organization, distinguish it from its competitors and enable it to implement a successful innovative strategy.

Unique abilities contribute to the collective knowledge shared among members of an organization, shaping their shared identity.

Among the elements characterizing distinctive skills are (1) the knowledge and skills of the human resources who operate in the organization, (2) the management systems that guide and control the knowledge creation processes, and (3) the values and norms that support knowledge.

The definition of the strategy cannot ignore the distinctive capabilities but must rather find the best way to exploit them for the purposes of affirming the competitive advantage.

The intensity of the strategic learning process generates (1) *incremental strategic learning*, (2) *radical strategic learning*, and (3) *consolidation strategic learning* (Kuwada, 1998; Vänttinen & Pyhältö, 2009). Both represent two different ways of developing the organization.

Incremental strategic learning constitutes a form of exploitation-stabilization of the adopted entrepreneurial formula. It allows the organization to reap the fruits of the business idea without radically changing the existing relationships between product and market. It is a form of learning that manifests itself through a continuous, voluntary, and conscious growth of knowledge as a result of experimentation and feedback processes without modifying the system of acquired knowledge.

Radical strategic learning is the basis of the creation of new development hypotheses and the new entrepreneurial formula. It generates from intuitions and beliefs that have not yet become new entrepreneurial visions. It is a form of learning that calls into question all the preexisting cognitive heritage.

Consolidation strategic learning is a form of mechanical, automatic learning that makes little use of the reflective and cognitive dimension (Abualqumboz et al., 2021). It manifests as a flexible adjustment in behavior, while the activity itself remains the same. It is a type of automatic learning where external information is absorbed without engaging any critical thinking processes. It leads to a strengthening of the information stored in a person's long-term memory.

In the literature, there exist two methods for advancing organizations, each implying distinct organizational learning processes that may either alternate over time or occur concurrently: (1) *consolidation-oriented learning* process and (2) *innovation-oriented learning* process.

Consolidation-oriented learning process represents a kind of natural way of development of organizations. They materialize in incremental innovation processes that give rise to consolidation, the articulation of the entrepreneurial formula, and the continuous improvement of efficiency and original distinctive skills. These circuits essentially aim at a dimensional development of the organization and its long-term survival (Siguaw et al., 2006).

Innovation-oriented learning process is observed more frequently after the organization has consolidated its basic strategic structure, and it can count on a critical mass sufficient to generate new resources and fuel new innovations. They possess a distinctly radical nature, as they focus on strengthening competitive advantage and minimizing the organization's reliance on external factors. The presence of creative products, novel ideas for utilizing present offerings, strong unique competencies, and the capacity to recognize external stimuli are essential prerequisites for effectively initiating a radical innovation process (Wilson et al., 2023).

3.5 Cognitive Style, Learning, and Innovation

The link between learning and innovation, and the consequent parallelism between innovative organization and learning organization, has deep roots in managerial literature (Rayner & Riding, 1997; Riding, 1997; Sadler-Smith & Badger, 1998).

Innovation is defined as an invention that has had commercial success, that is, it has found industrial application and has satisfied the latent and manifest needs of the consumer. It represents the ability to generate new behaviors in a proactive manner. Innovation implies the acquisition of new knowledge by the organization that produces an improving effect on the overall efficiency of the organization.

Part of the doctrine believes that decision-makers evaluate the risk connected to innovation based on their ability to learn and control uncertainty. The control of innovation risks represents a capacity that can be acquired through learning and enhanced in contexts close to experience. The innovative process is surrounded by uncertainty and risk: in fact, it is carried out in a probabilistic context for which it is not possible to know in advance whether a certain result can be achieved and whether it will be more successful on the market (Bhatti et al., 2020).

In general, four categories of innovations can be identified (Cafferata, 2007):

1. *Radical innovations*. They appear discontinuously in phases of strong economic depression. Radical innovation represents a technological leap that presupposes the application of new ideas that generate a widespread redefinition of the knowledge available to the organization.
2. *Marginal or incremental innovations*. These innovations appear continuously and with a frequency that varies from sector to sector, bringing improvements to the existing series of products or processes.
3. *New technological systems*, i.e., constellations of innovations, both radical and incremental, interrelated with each other.
4. *Technological revolutions* refer to profound transformations of technology with effects on the entire social system.

Innovation, viewed as a comprehensive process, requires a multicentered, cross-functional, and multidisciplinary approach to learning. This approach breaks down the isolation of corporate functions, enabling critical comparisons that foster integrated and widespread knowledge. As a result, we gain a deeper understanding of complex phenomena, initiating a learning process that embeds itself within the group and ultimately disseminates throughout the organization, minimizing the risks of failure. Individuals engaged in the innovation process must understand the developing challenges in various functional areas, beyond just their own. Additionally, they should possess the skills to address these problems, form effective working groups, and collaborate within those teams (Chen et al., 2018).

Innovation may stem from individual efforts, but true innovation arises from the collaborative endeavors of a team that integrates the finest human resources within the organization. This collective group utilizes knowledge, enhances its meaning, and extracts it from a theoretical framework that deviates from the conventional paradigms associated with the team. Often, these theories not only encompass but also advance beyond earlier concepts, making it highly improbable for a single individual to generate the innovative idea alone (Hayes & Allinson, 1998; Orieno et al., 2024).

Innovation is fostered by the presence of a conducive organizational atmosphere within companies. It promotes the exchange of extensive knowledge and inspires participants to tackle the challenges presented to them. Establishing and sustaining such an environment not only necessitates the presence of cooperative relationships among the generators, sponsors, and orchestrators of the innovation process but also it demands a distinct organizational structure. To achieve this goal, it is necessary to consider the establishment of an incentive system that, on the one hand, provides avenues for independent and innovative work and, on the other hand, rewards individuals who contribute to the creation and growth of new concepts by ensuring career progression and acknowledgment (both financial and nonfinancial) based on their efforts (Nonaka et al., 2014; Valeri, 2021).

3.6 Innovative Organization

The analysis carried out in the previous chapters has tried to show how the organization and its discipline have evolved in a parallel and continuous way in relation to the organization and its economic, social, and cultural reference context. Since the Industrial Revolution, society and economy have undergone radical changes, always posing new challenges and new goals to organizations (Mercurio, 2016). Organizations have proactively sought to adapt to the new reference contexts, striving to avoid experiencing these changes in a passive and "traumatic" manner. Instead, they aim to leverage these changes as opportunities for growth and success. Consequently, the organization is increasingly viewed as an open system that is in constant interaction with its external environment (Aramburu et al., 2015; Bhardwaj, 2020; Valeri & Baggio, 2021).

The economic and social scenario of the new millennium, primarily defined by ongoing and rapid technological advancements, has compelled companies to reassess their management and organizational structures to meet the new challenges presented by this context. This shift has implications for management control, the actual performance methods at work, and a heightened focus on employee motivation levels, all while keeping unchanged.

These new improvement techniques aim at reinterpreting the generality of the processes present in the value production chain according to an approach aimed at innovation, to make the organization competitive and successful on the market.

Innovation, therefore, emerges as the fundamental essence of corporate goals. From this viewpoint, as we have observed, the inclination toward collaboration and the value placed on human capital consistently rises, accompanied by a heightened focus on the significance of knowledge and its dissemination.

The best knowledge management not only requires the provision of technological tools (computers, social network, Intranet) suitable for ensuring its circulation but also the creation of a "business environment" that tends to knowledge training, sharing, and exchange.

It is essential to create a genuine organizational environment that takes advantage of the informal relationships that exist within it. In this setting, each member should recognize the importance of knowledge and learning, as well as the necessity for innovation and change that they collectively face alongside the organization itself. As a result, the need for flexibility and a willingness to cooperate become genuine priorities for individual members, driving them to enhance their efforts and collaboration.

Consequently, the environment of the organization should be defined by a culture of trust between management and employees, as well as by a supportive atmosphere for training and educational development. The requirement of "creativity" in the workers and in the management levels, which is considered as "a break in the routine," begins to be more and more important to the detriment of the scientific vision of the classical school.

Creativity serves as a crucial strategic asset since it underpins innovation. Indeed, innovation is shaped by a learning process that is intertwined with and bolstered by fresh ideas and new solutions (Amabile et al., 1996; Valaei et al., 2022).

The working environment and, in general, the organizational context have a relevant influence on the propensity of individuals toward creativity and innovative activities. Consequently, a contemporary organization must more frequently confront the necessity to reinvent itself, embracing a mindset of ongoing renewal and an inclination toward adaptability and flexibility.

Together with the concept of knowledge management, the model of the so-called learning organization begins to develop, an organizational structure that ensures the development of knowledge-generating practices and, consequently, better levels of response to the changes imposed by the external environment. The system that wants to become a learning organization must therefore be able to create shared knowledge, visions, and behavioral models, by enhancing the willingness to experiment and implement new insights, while learning from past experiences and those of others, to gain advantages and benefits from both the errors committed and the successes attained.

In a learning organization, learning and innovation are essential concepts that enable the accumulation of intellectual capital, which can then be transformed into a competitive edge. At the same time, collaboration, trust, and innovation are revealed as the key principles for shaping the modern organizational structure. Within the organization, the interplay between different contexts and components is pivotal, as these interaction areas are recognized as the foundation for generating knowledge in a learning organization (Von Krogh et al., 2012).

The organizational framework should align with these trends by systematically managing and distributing activities. It should view these activities as interconnected and mutually influential, instead of being seen as linear sequences dictated by cause and effect.

The fundamental idea is that any change within an organization can occur due to a collective readiness within its structure. Consequently, there is a need to "nurture" the mindset of individual members, which should have an encouraging and motivating influence on the environments where social interaction happens (Amar, 2004). In reality, dialogue is generated in these settings, along with the knowledge and interactions between the individual elements of the organization. An organization that successfully maps these relationships and interactions gains the benefit of more readily recognizing the boundaries and the necessity for intervention. This ability enables it to pinpoint issues more swiftly, thereby preventing resource waste, as it can effectively identify and address them.

In the learning organization, the continuous and constant accumulation and sharing of new knowledge is a fundamental element, to guarantee a shared, constant, and continuous learning process. The fundamental requirement for facilitating the learning process is that individual members possess the necessary tools and skills for effective learning. Indeed, learning is not simply an automatic process linked to the mere presence of information; rather, it is a carefully organized endeavor that necessitates a specific inclination and certain cognitive abilities.

As knowledge management systems advance, the notion of a learning organization is increasingly vital for organizational analysis, given that knowledge is now recognized as the foundation of competitiveness in the new economic and social landscape of the second millennium.

3.7 Learning-Oriented Organizations to Support Decision-Making

Learning-oriented organizations focused on learning function as a vibrant network of knowledge and a pool of skills that foster innovation through unpredictable routes and with an aim for transformation (Bonomi et al., 2019; Capaldo, 2014; Holm et al., 1996; Miles & Snow, 1986). Initially, there is a significant degree of integration among activities in a learning-oriented environment (Huysman, 2000; Short & Venkatraman, 1992; Sorenson et al., 2004).

Integration enables us to bridge the gaps caused by organizational hierarchies and insufficient technology in the production workflow. Integration involves a mutual dependence, ongoing interaction among activities, the establishment of an informal communication network, and persistent communication channels to enhance access to information resources (Baggio & Valeri, 2020; Brass et al., 2004; Vătămănescu et al., 2023).

In organizations focused on learning, the frameworks are established to facilitate innovative processes. Every form of innovation shifts the focus on the goals and overall effectiveness of the organizational system, which suffers from a lack of cohesion due to fragmented functions. The improvement of activities should be acknowledged by the entire organization, even if it pertains to specific operational units or functions (Al-Raqadi et al., 2017).

Organizational structures must be flexible to ensure efficient and effective governance of innovation processes. The hierarchy leaves room for wide margins of autonomy, the communication flow is intense, and it involves the entire hierarchical pyramid (not only top down but also bottom up). Organizational structures must be conceived as reservoirs of skills, or rather they must train and make available the required professionalism and guarantee methods, techniques, and tools.

Does Learning Ability Influence Decision-Making?

Decision-making framework that aids organizational leaders is shaped by their capacity to learn (Läpple & Barham, 2019). As a result, the notion that humans possess full knowledge of reality is discarded, leading to the need to manage the stimuli provided by the environment to the decision-maker. This process helps in identifying the information these stimuli represent, which ultimately varies from person to person. Frequently, the interpretation of specific information by outside parties can lead to a skewing of the probabilities linked to various actions taken by an individual, resulting in differing decisions made by different people. Decision-makers primarily act as selectors and interpreters of information based on the mental frameworks they possess (Bierly et al., 2000).

Deciding means choosing information on which to focus your interpretation based on your causal maps. The decision-maker pays attention and selects on the wealth of information as not all existing information is accessible to him and not all of it has equal significance for decision-making purposes (Palos & Veres Stancovici, 2016). The more problematic the decision-making situation is, the more necessary it is to resort to cognitive simplification processes which, through the selection of information guided by the decision-making experience gained, guarantees concentration on the relevant problematic aspects. Furthermore, in the implementation of decisions, a fundamental role is played by previous experience which helps decision-makers to identify the errors made and guide them in making the decision (Kucharska & Bedford, 2020; Machado & Davim, 2014).

In organization, learning represents the result of the feedback that knowledge operates on the organizational dimension of the decision-making process. In particular, the knowledge that derives from the implementation of the decision can modify the characteristics of the decision-making process by acting on the corporate culture (*double-loop learning*) or by determining an adjustment of organizational memory through a modification of the operational knowledge implicit in it (*single-loop learning*) (Argyris, 1977, 1999).

References

Abualqumboz, M., Chan, P. W., Bamford, D., & Reid, I. (2021). Temporal dimensions of knowledge exchanges in horizontal knowledge networks. *Journal of Knowledge Management, 25*(4), 899–919. https://doi.org/10.1108/JKM-05-2020-0346

Adler, P. S., & Heckscher, C. C. (Eds.). (2006). *The firm a collaborative community: Reconstructing trust in the knowledge economy*. Oxford University Press.

Allio, R. J. (2019). Becoming a leader—First, take charge of your own learning process. *Strategy & Leadership, 46*(3), 21–28.

Al-Raqadi, A. M. S., Abdul, R. A., Masrom, M., & Al-Riyami, B. S. N. (2017). Enhancing transparency and learning sustainability on the perceptions of improving naval ships' support performance. *International Journal of Systems Assurance Engineering and Management, 8*(1), 265–289.

Amabile, T. M., Conti, R., Coon, H., Lazenby, J., & Herron, M. (1996). Assessing the work environment for creativity. *Academy of Management Journal, 39*, 1154–1184.

Amar, A. D. (2004). Motivating knowledge workers to innovate: A model integrating motivation dynamics and antecedents. *European Journal of Innovation Management, 7*(2), 89–101.

Aramburu, N., Saenz, J., & Blanco, C. (2015). Structural capital, innovation capability, and company performance in technology-based Colombian firms. *Cuadernos de Gestion, 15*(1), 39–60.

Ardichvili, A., Page, V., & Wentling, T. (2003). Motivation and barriers to participation in virtual knowledge-sharing communities of practice. *Journal of Knowledge Management, 7*(1), 64–77. https://doi.org/10.1108/13673270310463626

Argote, L. (2013). *Organizational learning. Creating, retaining and transferring knowledge* (2nd ed.). Springer.

Argyris, C. (1977). Double loop learning in organizations. *Harvard Business Review, 55*(5), 115–125.

Argyris, C. (1999). *On organizational learning*. Oxford University Press.

Austin, J. R. (2003). Transactive memory in organizational groups: The effects of content, consensus, specialization, and accuracy on group performance. *Journal of Applied Psychology, 88*(5), 866–878. https://doi.org/10.1037/0021-9010.88.5.866

Baggio, R., & Valeri, M. (2020). Network science and sustainable performance of family businesses in tourism. *Journal of Family Business Management, 12*, 200. https://doi.org/10.1108/JFBM-06-2020-0048

Balle, A. R., Oliveira, M., & Curado, C. M. M. (2020). Knowledge sharing and absorptive capacity: Interdependency and complementarity. *Journal of Knowledge Management, 24*(8), 1943–1964. https://doi.org/10.1108/JKM-12-2019-0666

Bhardwaj, B. R. (2020). Influence of knowledge management on product innovation by intrapreneurial firms. *Global Knowledge, Memory and Communication, 69*(1/2), 38–57.

Bhatti, S. H., Zakariya, R., Vrontis, D., Santoro, G., & Christofi, M. (2020). High-performance work systems, innovation and knowledge sharing: An empirical analysis in the context of project-based organizations. *Employee Relations, 43*(2), 438–458.

Bierly, P. E., Kessler, E. H., & Christensen, E. W. (2000). Organizational learning, knowledge and wisdom. *Journal of Organizational Change Management, 13*(6), 595–618. https://doi.org/10.1108/09534810010378605

Boden, A., Nett, B., von Rekowski, T., & Wulf, V. (2012). Strategic learning. In N. M. Seel (Ed.), *Encyclopedia of the sciences of learning*. Springer. https://doi.org/10.1007/978-1-4419-1428-6_460

Bolisani, E., & Bratianu, C. (2018). The emergence of knowledge management. In *Emergent knowledge strategies* (Knowledge management and organizational learning) (Vol. 4). Springer. https://doi.org/10.1007/978-3-319-60657-6_2

Bonomi, S., Sarti, D., & Torre, T. (2019). Creating a collaborative network for welfare services in the public sector. A knowledge-based perspective. *Journal of Business Research, 112*, 440–449. https://doi.org/10.1016/j.jbusres.2019.11.050

Bontis, N. (1999). Managing organizational knowledge by diagnosing intellectual capital: Framing and advancing the state of the field. *International Journal of Technology Management, 18*(5/6/7/8), 433–462. https://doi.org/10.1504/IJTM.1999.002780

Bood, R., & Postma, T. (1997). Strategic learning with scenarios. *European Management Journal, 15*(6), 633–647. https://doi.org/10.1016/S0263-2373(97)00047-9

Brass, D. G., Galaskiewicz, J., Greve, H. R., & Tsai, W. (2004). Taking stock of networks and organizations: A multilevel perspective. *Academy of Management Journal, 47*(6), 795–817. https://doi.org/10.5465/20159624

Cafferata, R. (2007). *Direzione e Organizzazione Aziendale*. Aracne.

Capaldo, A. (2014). Network governance: A cross-level study of social mechanisms, knowledge benefits, and strategic outcomes in joint-design alliances. *Industrial Marketing Management, 43*(4), 685–703. https://doi.org/10.1016/j.indmarman.2014.02.002

Chen, Y. T., Liou, S., & Chen, L. F. (2018). The relationships among gender, cognitive styles, learning strategies, and learning performance in the flipped classroom. *International Journal of Human–Computer Interaction, 35*(4–5), 395–403. https://doi.org/10.1080/10447318.2018.1543082

Cohen, W. M., & Levinthal, D. A. (1990). Absorptive capacity: A new perspective on learning and innovation. *Administrative Science Quarterly, 35*(1), 128–152. https://doi.org/10.2307/2393553

Donate, M. J., & De Pablo, J. D. S. (2015). The role of knowledge-oriented leadership in knowledge management practices and innovation. *Journal of Business Research, 68*(2), 360–370. https://doi.org/10.1016/j.jbusres.2014.06.022

Eisenhardt, K. M., & Zbaracki, M. J. (1992). Strategic decision making. *Strategic Management Journal, 13*, 17–37. https://doi.org/10.1002/smj.4250130904

Foss, N. J. (1999). The competence-based approach: Veblenian ideas in the contemporary theory of the firm. *Cambridge Journal of Economics, 3*, 127–144.

Gallupe, B. (2001). Knowledge management systems: Surveying the landscape. *International Journal of Management Reviews, 3*, 61–77. https://doi.org/10.1111/1468-2370.00054

Hayes, J., & Allinson, C. W. (1998). Cognitive style and the theory and practice of individual and collective learning in organizations. *Human Relations, 51*, 847–871. https://doi.org/10.1023/A:1016978926688

Hecker, A. (2012). Knowledge beyond the individual? Making sense of a notion of collective knowledge in organization theory. *Organization Studies, 33*(3), 423. https://doi.org/10.1177/0170840611433995

Hedlund, G. (1994). A model of knowledge management and the N-form corporation. *Strategic Management Journal, 14*, 73–90. https://doi.org/10.1002/smj.4250151006

Holm, D., Eriksson, K., & Johanson, J. (1996). Business networks and cooperation in international business relationships. *Journal of International Business Studies, 27*, 1033–1053. https://doi.org/10.1057/palgrave.jibs.8490162

Huysman, M. (2000). An organizational learning approach to the learning organization. *European Journal of Work and Organizational Psychology, 9*(2), 133–145. https://doi.org/10.1080/135943200397905

Jasimuddin, S. M. (2008). A holistic view of knowledge management strategy. *Journal of Knowledge Management, 12*(2), 57–66. https://doi.org/10.1108/13673270810859514

King, W. R. (2001). Strategies for creating a learning organization. *Information Systems Management, 18*(1), 12–20. https://doi.org/10.1201/1078/43194.18.1.20010101/31261.3

Kucharska, W., & Bedford, D. A. D. (2020). Love your mistakes!—They help you adapt to change. How do knowledge, collaboration and learning cultures foster organizational intelligence? *Journal of Organizational Change Management, 33*(7), 1329–1354. https://doi.org/10.1108/JOCM-02-2020-0052

Kuntz, R. D., & Matta, N. (2002). *Knowledge management and organizational memories*. Springer.

Kuwada, K. (1998). Strategic learning: The continuous side of discontinuous strategic change. *Organization Science, 9*(6), 719–736. https://doi.org/10.1287/orsc.9.6.719

Läpple, D., & Barham, B. L. (2019). How do learning ability, advice from experts and peers shape decision making? *Journal of Behavioral and Experimental Economics, 80*, 92–107. https://doi.org/10.1016/j.socec.2019.03.010

Lee, J. D., & Kirlik, A. (2013). *The Oxford handbook of cognitive engineering*. Oxford University Press.

Loermans, J. (2002). Synergizing the learning organization and knowledge management. *Journal of Knowledge Management, 6*(3), 285–294. https://doi.org/10.1108/13673270210434386

Machado, C., & Davim, J. P. (2014). *Organizational learning, learning organization and knowledge creation and transmission: Some reflections*. Wiley Publishing. https://doi.org/10.1002/9781119005117.ch9

Maheshwari, S. K., & Yadav, J. (2019). The role of HR in leadership development. *Development and Learning in Organizations, 33*(5), 20–23.

Mercurio, R. (2016). *Organizational networks for innovation*. Egea.

Miles, R. E., & Snow, C. C. (1986). Networks organizations: New concepts for new forms. *California Management Review, 28*(3), 62–75. https://doi.org/10.2307/41165202

Mintzberg, H. (1987). The strategy concept I: Five Ps for strategy. *California Management Review, 30*(1), 11. https://doi.org/10.2307/41165263

Moon, H., Ruona, W., & Valentine, T. (2017). Organizational strategic learning capability: Exploring the dimensions. *European Journal of Training and Development, 41*(3), 222–240. https://doi.org/10.1108/EJTD-08-2016-0061

Newman, N., & Newman, D. (2015). Learning and knowledge: A dream or nightmare for employees. *The Learning Organization, 22*(1), 58–71. https://doi.org/10.1108/TLO-02-2013-0002

Nonaka, I., & Takeuchi, H. (1995). *The knowledge—Creating company: How Japanese companies create the dynamics of innovation*. Oxford University Press.

Nonaka, I., Takeuchi, H., & Umemoto, K. (2014). A theory of organizational knowledge creation. *International Journal of Technology Management, 11*(7–8), 833–845. https://doi.org/10.1504/IJTM.1996.025472

Normann, R. (2001). *Reframing business. When the map changes the landscape*. John Wiley & Sons.

Oluikpe, P. (2012). Developing a corporate knowledge management strategy. *Journal of Knowledge Management, 16*(6), 862–878. https://doi.org/10.1108/13673271211276164

Orieno, O. H., Udeh, C. A., Oriekhoe, O. I., Odonkor, B., & Ndubuisi, N. L. (2024). Innovative management strategies in contemporary organizations: A review: Analyzing the evolution and impact of modern management practices, with an emphasis on leadership, organizational culture, and change management. *International Journal of Management & Entrepreneurship Research, 6*(1), 167–190.

Palos, R., & Veres Stancovici, V. (2016). Learning in organization. *The Learning Organization, 23*(1), 2–22. https://doi.org/10.1108/TLO-01-2015-0001

Rayner, S., & Riding, R. (1997). Towards a categorisation of cognitive styles and learning styles. *Educational Psychology, 17*(1–2), 5–27. https://doi.org/10.1080/0144341970170101

Riding, R. J. (1997). On the nature of cognitive style. *Educational Psychology, 17*(1–2), 29–49. https://doi.org/10.1080/0144341970170102

Sadler-Smith, E., & Badger, B. (1998). Cognitive style, learning and innovation. *Technology Analysis & Strategic Management, 10*(2), 247–266. https://doi.org/10.1080/09537329808524314

Senge, P. (1990). *Fifth discipline: The art and practice of the learning organisation*. Century.

Short, J. E., & Venkatraman, N. (1992). Beyond business process redesign: Redefining Baxter's business network. *Sloan Management Review, 34*(1), 7.

Siguaw, J. A., Simpson, P. M., & Enz, C. A. (2006). Conceptualizing innovation orientation: A framework for study and integration of innovation research. *Journal of Product Innovation Management, 23*(6), 556–574. https://doi.org/10.1111/j.1540-5885.2006.00224.x

Sorenson, O., Rivkin, J., & Fleming, L. (2004). Complexity, networks and knowledge flow. *Research Policy, 33*(10), 1615–1634. https://doi.org/10.1016/j.respol.2006.05.002

Sun, H. C. (2003). Conceptual clarifications for 'organizational learning', 'learning organization' and 'a learning organization. *Human Resource Development International, 6*(2), 153–166. https://doi.org/10.1080/13678860110086465

Usai, A., Pironti, M., Mital, M., & Aouina Mejri, C. (2018). Knowledge discovery out of text data: A systematic review via text mining. *Journal of Knowledge Management, 22*, 1471–1488. https://doi.org/10.1108/JKM-11-2017-0517

Usman, Z. M., & Musa, M. A. (2012). The influence of organizational knowledge sharing on employee motivation. In *International conference on information retrieval & knowledge management* (pp. 87–90).

Valaei, N., Rezaei, S., Bressolles, G., & Dent, M. M. (2022). Indispensable components of creativity, innovation, and FMCG companies' competitive performance: A resource-based view (RBV) of the firm. *Asia-Pacific Journal of Business Administration, 14*(1), 1–26. https://doi.org/10.1108/APJBA-11-2020-0420

Valeri, M. (2021). *Organizational studies. Implications for the strategic management*. Springer.

Valeri, M. (2024). *Knowledge management and knowledge sharing. Business strategies and an emerging theoretical field*. Springer. https://doi.org/10.1007/978-3-031-37868-3

Valeri, M., & Baggio, R. (2021). Increasing the efficiency of knowledge transfer in Italian tourism system: A network approach. *Current Issues in Tourism, 25*(13), 2127–2142. https://doi.org/10.1080/13683500.2021.1937960

Van Zolingen, S. J., Streumer, J. N., & Stooker, M. (2001). Problems in knowledge management: A case study of a knowledge-intensive company. *International Journal of Training and Development, 5*, 168–184. https://doi.org/10.1111/1468-2419.00130

Vänttinen, M., & Pyhältö, K. (2009). Strategy process as an innovative learning environment. *Management Decision, 47*(5), 778 791. https://doi.org/10.1108/00251740910960114

Vătămănescu, E.-M., Bratianu, C., Dabija, D.-C., & Popa, S. (2023). Capitalizing online knowledge networks: From individual knowledge acquisition towards organizational achievements. *Journal of Knowledge Management, 27*(5), 1366–1389. https://doi.org/10.1108/JKM-04-2022-0273

Von Krogh, G., Nonaka, I., & Rechsteiner, L. (2012). Leadership in organizational knowledge creation: A review and framework. *Journal of Management Studies, 19*(1), 240–277. https://doi.org/10.1111/j.1467-6486.2010.00978.x

Walczak, S. (2005). Organizational knowledge management structure. *The Learning Organization, 12*(4), 330–339. https://doi.org/10.1108/09696470510599118

Wilson, G. A., Case, T., & Dobni, C. B. (2023). A global study of innovation-oriented firms: Dimensions, practices, and performance. *Technological Forecasting and Social Change, 187*, 122257. https://doi.org/10.1016/j.techfore.2022.122257

Zhang, X., & Wang, X. (2021). Team learning in interdisciplinary research teams: Antecedents and consequences. *Journal of Knowledge Management, 25*(6), 1429–1455. https://doi.org/10.1108/JKM-07-2019-0372

Knowledge Governance

4

4.1 Knowledge Management: Theories and Concepts

Knowledge encompasses information that is documented, published, or captured in formats such as audio, video, and technical data, along with other intellectual property deemed by the organization to provide a strategic or tactical edge. It requires teamwork and collaboration among various levels within the organization to reach the desired objectives (Awad, 2007).

Knowledge management refers to the organized approach aimed at comprehending how knowledge is generated and administered. It involves examining and analyzing the methodologies employed by an organization to improve its effectiveness concerning knowledge and to secure consistent returns from its inventory of knowledge resources, which are maintained in a present state through ongoing renewal and updates (Wiig, 1997).

The process of managing knowledge can be made more fluid and effective through the integration of organizational and technological strategies aimed at improving collaboration with a system. This system can be seen as a complex network of both internal and external relationships that cannot be rigidly imposed or strictly standardized (Antonelli, 2013; Lazzeretti et al., 2019; Valeri & Baggio, 2020a, 2020b, 2021).

To achieve outstanding outcomes, individuals or organizations tasked with managing knowledge must possess the skills and understanding necessary to comprehend the knowledge resources they hold. This comprehension allows them to utilize these resources appropriately, drawing upon their subject matter expertise developed through years of experience in the field (Baggio & Valeri, 2020; Innocenti & Lazzeretti, 2019; Valeri, 2016).

Knowledge management aims to empower the organization to optimize the worth of all its information, intellectual property assets (such as patents, copyrights, technical know-how, trade secrets, etc.), and other pertinent knowledge resources

M. Valeri, *Organizations and Knowledge Management*, Knowledge Management and Organizational Learning 16, https://doi.org/10.1007/978-3-031-97954-5_4

through ongoing enhancement and replenishment, ensuring it stays relevant and valuable for the future (Simon, 1976). The relationship between an organization's business goals and knowledge management needs to be articulated clearly to allow the organization to efficiently and effectively manage its knowledge assets. This is essential for the organization to maintain competitiveness and adaptability in its market and industry, ultimately enabling it to benefit from market opportunities (Savage, 1990).

For knowledge to expand, it must be disseminated and exchanged among the employees, partners, and other stakeholders of the organization, as they contribute their own insights, enhancing the overall knowledge base. This process results in "on-demand" availability of essential information, which is crucial for maintaining competitive effectiveness (Janis & Mann, 1977). Organizations are presently modifying their corporate frameworks to align more closely with the unique requirements of knowledge management, aiming to achieve optimal results from it (Cameron & Quinn, 2011).

The significance of knowledge has been recognized throughout human history. Nearly every kingdom and empire were constructed upon the foundation of knowledge, revered by the ruling class who employed it to legitimize their authority and dominance. Empires have been supplanted by organizations and corporations, yet this mindset has largely remained the same.

Organizations that have successfully commercialized their intellectual assets are capable of driving innovation, which serves as the engine powering the business landscape. Knowledge is the sole resource that expands when shared, and organizations that maintain their knowledge resources current and vibrant can surpass their rivals in the marketplace and cross the finish line ahead (Böhme & Stehr, 1986).

A key figure in management theory, Drucker (1993), remarked that knowledge is initially perceived as something to be utilized, envisioned as a resource and a utility for the future. The application of knowledge, such as the basic principles of levers and simple machines, was crucial in creating the motivation to develop machinery and mechanisms that triggered the Industrial Revolution. The impact of the Industrial Revolution brought significant changes, resulting in a remarkable increase in productivity, commonly known as the productivity evolution (Drucker, 1993).

The period after the major conflicts of World War 1 and World War 2 significantly influenced the nature of knowledge, leading to what is known as the "management revolution." This shift was marked by the development of various management theories and models proposed by scholars like Taylor, Fayol, and Mayo, aimed at improving the productivity of nonworker employees. Since knowledge was the cornerstone of these transformations, it quickly came to be seen as a resource of significant worth, akin to gold, crude oil, steel, and coal, given that the future of organizations relies on it (Drucker, 1993).

4.2 Knowledge Management and Impact on Organizational Design

Skills-based human resource management stems from the necessity for organizations to establish a new approach to the management and development of their human resources, particularly in an environment where the structure of organizations and the key factors for success have significantly changed.

As a result, we are observing occurrences like the flattening of organizational structures, a focus on core business operations that has progressively fostered extensive network dynamics, the self-management of resources, and an ongoing reassessment of activities due to advancements in information and communication technology (Shu-hsien Liao, 2003; Milton et al., 1999).

In an intricate economic landscape, the importance of knowledge has significantly impacted the way work activities are redefined. Indeed, we are observing a shift from work being seen solely as a task-oriented activity to work being viewed as an exercise of intelligence, given the significantly higher intellectual demands of tasks that are now more hands-on than they used to be (Bhatt, 2001; Gold et al., 2001). Learning, defined as the process of assigning meaning to data and information, serves as a strategic foundation for work. What is truly important in work organization is not mastering a lifelong skill or simply adhering to the demands of efficiency; instead, it is about cultivating the ability to innovate and generate new ideas. Interruption will take precedence over persistence, randomness will overshadow replication, irregularity will surpass the standard, and the temporary initiative will dominate routine (Collis, 1996; Garavelli et al., 2004; Oluikpe, 2012).

Being proficient today is less about having a reservoir of knowledge and more about effectively navigating complex scenarios by utilizing the available resources of the organization in the most suitable manner. It also involves tapping into a diverse range of knowledge. The skills, abilities, and responsibilities assigned to an individual are no longer predetermined; instead, they are constantly reshaped and reinvented based on the evolving relationship between the individual and their environment.

It is essential to enhance the focus on addressing issues, which is reflected in the capacity to foster innovation during work tasks within the organization. Nonetheless, both learning and innovation necessitate sufficient freedom for independent thought and inventive approaches to tackle challenges that arise during work. The ability to select fresh approaches for tackling both new and existing challenges is what enables us to produce new knowledge and, consequently, create new value (Fugate et al., 2009; Noruzy et al., 2013).

The application of outdated management and development tools for assessing skills is not well suited for accurately understanding the ongoing changes in the described situation. Skills management was developed with the purpose of assessing and acknowledging the acquisition of essential knowledge necessary for competition.

Knowledge management is a resource designed to assist individuals in cultivating essential skills, identifying shortcomings, and offering foundational information for facilitating learning. After identifying the essential knowledge for competitiveness and assessing both individual and collective levels of acquisition, the challenge becomes figuring out how to convert vital skills into organizational learning (Argyris & Schon, 1978; Fiol & Lyles, 1985; Huber, 1991).

A key element of the managerial literature concerning knowledge management addresses the essential issue of the epistemological dualism that influences the entire discussion regarding the essence of knowledge.

In this context, Nonaka and Takeuchi (1995) present two approaches on knowledge: the subjectivist perspective, which regards knowledge as a specific and concrete phenomenon closely connected to the cognitive experiences of the individual, and the objectivist perspective, which views knowledge as a general and abstract entity that exists independently of the individual acquiring it.

The first perspective defines knowing as the ability to accurately describe an object of knowledge as it truly is, without regard to the individual's beliefs, cultural influences, or social background. In contrast, the second perspective views knowing as the act of shaping what is known and creating the necessary conditions for its presence.

A careful analysis of Nonaka and Takeuchi's work reveals the fundamental principles that support the growth of organizations focused on fostering knowledge creation and its subsequent sharing.

Recognizing that conventional organizational frameworks lack the flexibility needed to perform all these roles, Nonaka and Takeuchi (1995) pinpoint the hypertextual organization as the structure that can address the shortcomings of both hierarchical systems and task forces. Apart from the visual appeal of the hypertextual analogy, the practical significance of the authors' suggestion is undoubtedly at the forefront of contemporary organizational development models.

The hypertextual organizational framework is designed to serve as a structural basis for knowledge generation within the organization. It facilitates the ongoing gathering, development, and utilization of knowledge through an iterative process focused on interconnected organizational pathways and environments (Daft & Weick, 1984).

The hypertextual organizational framework primarily facilitates the portrayal of an organizational environment that can not only transcend the inherent inflexibilities typical of any structure but also adopt adaptive and flexible behaviors (Weick, 1979).

The organization of internal roles and specialties aligns with the organization of knowledge within organizations. The focus on specific sectors complicates the acquisition of comprehensive knowledge and necessitates the essential integration of various forms of understanding (Darroch, 2003; March, 1988; Sahlin-Andersson & Engwall, 2002).

Another key element is the necessity to establish environments for interaction and idea exchange: knowledge cannot be generated without the capacity or opportunity to foster positive communication and relational exchanges. This applies both to the organizational setting that enables such interactions and to the values and linguistic frameworks required for knowledge transfer and the creation of new understanding. In this context, the writers focus on the use of figurative and symbolic language, which refers to the capacity to convey implicit and unspoken knowledge through analogies or imagery.

Metaphor serves as a valuable tool for conveying implicit knowledge, which is the type of understanding that is hard to articulate through formal language. It relies on the evocative strength of imagery to communicate and disseminate ideas that would otherwise be challenging to express. However, metaphors and imagery, as long as they do not distort essential information, are a highly practical application of language.

By making comparisons within the team and employing figurative language, individuals can connect the emerging concepts to the broader body of knowledge. Another fundamental aspect of the organizational framework proposed by Nonaka and Takeuchi (1995) pertains to the individuals involved in the knowledge creation process.

While it is common within organizational culture to believe that the directions taken by an organization stem solely from the leader's visionary abilities, the authors acknowledge the important contribution of middle management to the development of knowledge.

This managerial model, far different from the most well-known managerial models, is called middle-up-down. While the traditional hierarchical and participatory model does not fully favor the complex process of knowledge conversion, i.e., socialization, combination, externalization, and internalization, the middle-up-down model instead favors both the creation of new ideas and their diffusion.

4.3 Knowledge Networks and Communities of Practice

While Nonaka and Takeuchi's approach (1995) has its roots in Eastern thought and is associated with contemporary interest in knowledge management, the Western perspective introduces the concept of communities of practice and its relationship with organizational learning, largely influenced by the significant contributions of Orr (1990). In line with this perspective, knowledge is viewed as a subjective aspect. Knowledge is not contained within the person alone but exists within the network of relationships and social interactions that an individual has with their reference communities.

What defines a community? It has been characterized in various manners. Nonetheless, these descriptions all share a common element that spans from a basic mutual interest to the exchange of cognitive frameworks and shared identities (Davenport & Hall, 2002). Specifically, the casual and voluntary aspect of communities of practice has led to the chance to entrust informal networks with the responsibility of generating, sharing, and articulating the practical knowledge that individuals develop through their operational tasks (Brown & Duguid, 1991).

In this manner, the role of management is twofold: firstly, to acknowledge and facilitate the informal networks that stem from individuals' inherent desire for social interaction and, secondly, to develop protective measures that can harness knowledge as it is organically and spontaneously generated, before disseminating it throughout the organization.

Research, studies, and the use of information systems that integrate organizational elements with knowledge management concerns are converging on the concept of a community of practice (Aljuwaiber, 2016; Bolisani & Scarso, 2014; Pattinson & Preece, 2014). This realm encompasses a convergence of experiential insights and theoretical reflections that outline new dimensions of competitive growth, emphasizing the significance of internal capabilities to foster innovation, a crucial necessity in today's landscape to navigate ever-evolving and challenging markets.

Etienne Wenger (1988) was the first to describe the concept of a community of practice around the late 1990s, with two main goals in mind: to create a theory that framed learning is fundamentally a social phenomenon and, simultaneously, to offer a design tool that addressed issues related to corporate organization and training.

As suggest by Wenger et al. (2002, p. 4), "Communities of practice are groups of people who share a concern, a set of problems, or a passion about a topic, and who deepen their knowledge and expertise in this area by interacting on an ongoing basis."

Communities of practice, as acknowledged in the realm of international cooperation, voluntary organizations, scientific research groups, and generally among highly skilled individuals collaborating toward a shared organizational goal, demonstrate their ability to attain remarkable levels of operational efficiency within their specific areas of expertise. The underlying cause of this lies in the ability of communities to sustain themselves over time by actively renewing their cultural identity, continually learning among their members, and being willing to revise their own ways of understanding when those approaches are found to be flawed or unsuitable for reaching their shared objectives. This occurs through a collective enhancement that cannot simply be reduced to the individual processes of each member, as Wenger suggests (1988).

The ability to achieve such a goal of efficiency and competitiveness presupposes:

1. *Shared repertoire*: The relationship between practice and community generates a set of knowledge, tools, artifacts, and development processes that convey collective knowledge and preserve the memory of the community itself.
2. *Common initiatives*: This dimension focuses on the formation of a shared image of the problems and viable alternatives, the creation of objectives and priorities negotiated among members, and the development of a common awareness of tasks (Kukami & Armstrong, 2009).
3. *Commitment to reciprocity*: This dimension focuses on community context of individuals at work. They and their practices assume a recognition as part of something larger, which in turn is recognized as part of something that gives meaning to the work, the organization. Along this emotional dimension, individuals interact and share the experience that is specific to each of them, with the aim of nurturing collective learning (Immordino-Yang et al., 2019).

These prerequisites are driven by essential dynamics examined within the realms of philosophy, sociology, and anthropology. This refers to the procedure of semantic negotiation. The way facts and issues are understood, along with personal experiences and the shared, negotiated meanings within a community of practice, has shifted from being an individual cultural legacy to a collective cultural legacy.

Throughout the lifespan of any community of practice, the members involved are motivated to preserve and, when possible, enhance their personal background of experiences. This enables them to empathetically relate their experiences to those of their fellow members, leading to solutions that, while not fully embraced by everyone, serve as effective tools for the benefit of the entire community.

Diverse experiences and perspectives, contributed by various people within the same community, are often overlooked due to emotional and psychological factors, as well as logical and linguistic dynamics, which cannot be ignored or minimized in any way.

The characterization of a specific *knowledge acquisition* strategy is complicated (Böhme & Stehr, 1986; Fletcher & Harris, 2012; Gruber, 1989; Pellegrino & McNaughton, 2015). The notion of community of practice allows us to outline the contours of this domain within a model aimed at valorizing all those components that can be traced back to abstract relationships between theoretical concepts: within this model, the field of experience, in which the exchange between skills takes place, becomes the true focus of the *knowledge engineer* (Wielinga et al., 1992).

Frequently, people within the same corporate environment, who work toward a shared objective, organize and frame their contributions according to guidelines, protocols, and procedures established by higher management. These impositions frequently fail to address the actual issues at hand, are not readily applicable, and ultimately prove to be unproductive. Selection of a particular language to articulate and depict one's area of intervention is linked to the level of comprehension and necessitates thorough and genuine contemplation on one's own intervention strategies.

The extensive journey of developing a language that represents reality tends to accelerate the exchange of information and makes it easier for individuals to effectively compare their perspectives to address a shared issue. The concept of communities of practice, viewed as a methodological instrument for knowledge management, offers a valuable framework for transforming practice into an optimal network of interrelated meanings. Wenger's theory (1988), which establishes a complex system of experiences at the foundational structure of community learning, allows for a significant reevaluation of the influence of noncognitive elements in the semantic process of negotiations.

4.4 Implementing Knowledge Management Strategies

According to Bratianu (2022), *generic knowledge strategies* are approaches to knowledge management that can be tailored and applied within any organization based on its specific needs and adaptive capabilities. Fixed the intangible nature of knowledge resources and their nonlinear features, Porter's generic strategies cannot be directly utilized in the context of knowledge (Bolisani & Bratianu, 2018; Grant, 1996; Spender, 1996; Sveiby, 2001).

They ought to be considered from an alternate viewpoint. There are two viewpoints to consider: (a) the dynamics of organizational knowledge (Bratianu, 2011) and (b) the matrix of *known-unknowns* (Dalkir, 2005). The organizational knowledge dynamics (OKD) model is founded on the systems thinking approach as described by Jackson (2019). The aim of this analysis is to pinpoint the key variables that affect the dynamics of knowledge levels within the organization and to explore ways to manage these factors from a strategic viewpoint while keeping as it is. The factors involved include knowledge generation, knowledge gathering, knowledge depletion, knowledge transmission via the system's interface, and the sharing of knowledge.

The *known-unknown* matrix (Dalkir, 2005) is a generalized framework of that discussion, structuring the tension between what is known and what could be known regarding a problem or situation. Figure 4.1 depicts the system's knowledge states along with the relevant strategies designed to supply the knowledge resources necessary for the firm to attain a sustainable competitive edge.

These states of knowledge include both explicit and implicit knowledge. Explicit knowledge is rational and comes from the conscious part of the brain, allowing us to recognize the depth of our comprehension regarding a specific topic. However, tacit knowledge is influenced by the cognitive unconscious, which renders it nearly impossible for us to measure our own understanding (Damasio, 2012; Lakoff & Johnson, 1999).

This tacit knowledge is a kind of *known-unknown*. In addition to tacit knowledge being viewed as a conscious unknown, it also represents a lack of knowledge about unknowns in the external environment, particularly when we talk about the future and its inherent uncertainties.

In a finite world of knowledge and deterministic thinking, *known-unknowns* represent the knowledge domain we know, and we can make use of it. It is the interpretation of the metaphor used to explain how our brain is like a container where knowledge is accumulated through learning.

Strategy of Knowledge Exploitation

Knowledge serves as a strategic asset, yet it is generated and possessed by individual people (Davenport & Prusak, 2000; Polanyi, 1962, 1983; Russell, 2009). In organizations, knowledge can be combined and organized to create a shared understanding referred to as organizational knowledge.

In managerial literature, two interpretations of this concept are identified. The *restrictive* definition pertains to the knowledge that is possessed by the organization. It refers to the knowledge integrated within regulations, operational procedures, intellectual property laws, organizational culture, databases, and software systems. Edvinsson (2002) stated that it is the knowledge retained within an organization

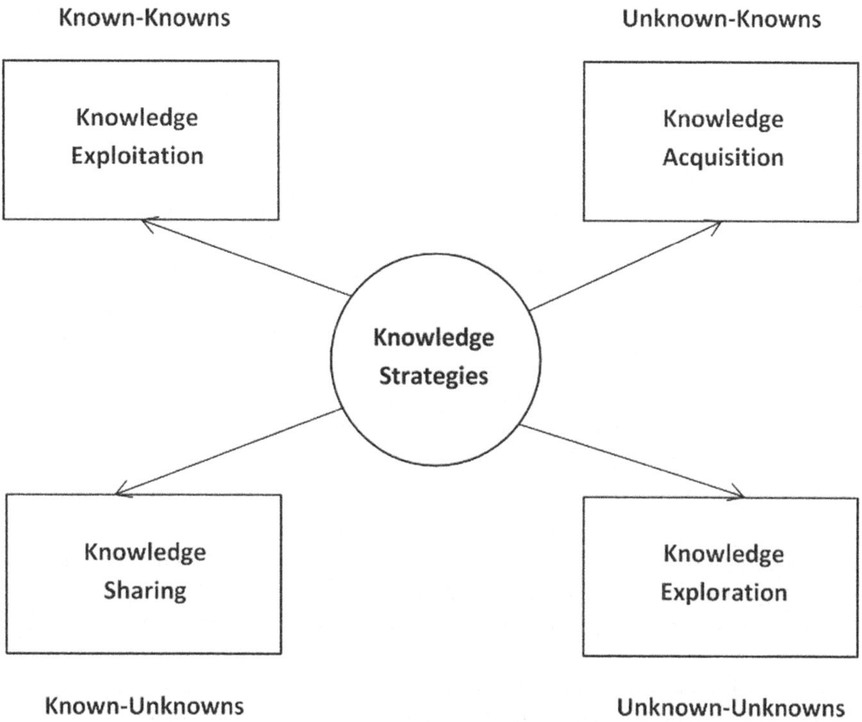

Fig. 4.1 Generic knowledge strategies. Source: Bratianu (2022)

after all employees have departed for the day. The organization possesses and governs it. *Extensive* organizational knowledge encompasses the complete scope of information, including the expertise held by employees. For organizations that rely heavily on knowledge, all types of organizational knowledge serve as a crucial strategic asset (Brown & Duguid, 1998).

The knowledge of individuals is integrated into organizational knowledge by *organizational integrators*: technology, managers, leaders, and organizational culture. Technology establishes particular frameworks that bring people together to engage in intricate tasks. According to Bratianu (2013), managers, leaders, and organizational culture function as nonlinear integrators, as they establish frameworks that incorporate knowledge in all its various forms, including rational, emotional, and spiritual dimensions. At the organizational level, integrated knowledge, along with various other intangible assets, forms the intellectual capital of the organization (Andriessen, 2004; Ricceri, 2008). The approach of knowledge utilization emphasizes the observable elements of organizational knowledge and makes efficient use of them to reach the organization's goals. As March (1991, p. 71) emphasizes, "exploitation includes such things as refinement, choice, production, efficiency, selection, implementation, execution." While we discuss on knowledge exploitation and knowledge exploration as distinct strategies, in reality, numerous organizations implement them together. Some authors call this ability to combine these strategies *the quality of organizational ambidexterity* (Andriopoulos & Lewis, 2009; Raisch et al., 2009).

Strategy of Knowledge Acquisition

Knowledge acquisition denotes the process of obtaining information from outside sources or through network interactions. When an organization lacks the capacity to internally develop the necessary knowledge through research, knowledge acquisition serves as a substitute for knowledge creation (Chaston & Mangles, 2000; Hoe & McShane, 2010). Knowledge acquisition is particularly utilized by SMEs when they lack the necessary time and/or financial resources to cultivate their own expertise (Chan & Chao, 2008; Durst & Edvardson, 2012). Knowledge acquisition primarily pertains to rational knowledge, as emotional and spiritual understanding tends to be developed internally.

Knowledge acquisition can take many forms, including acquiring research journals and international databases, buying software and artificial intelligence applications, engaging training programs and consultancy expertise, obtaining knowledge through network exchanges, and employing seasoned experts with extensive experience and skills.

From a broader viewpoint, the process of acquiring knowledge signifies the understanding that interacts with the external business environment (Liao et al., 2010). Organizations typically obtain knowledge by acquiring intellectual property rights, such as patents, to apply new technologies for the development of innovative products and services.

In the literature, the knowledge acquisition strategy is also called the *knowledge capturing* process (Clark et al., 2008; Eucker, 2007; Milton, 2007). Knowledge capturing emphasizes the retrieval of valuable insights from specialists and the integration of that knowledge into databases and AI applications. It is an intricate and specialized procedure aimed at facilitating the development of *expert systems* and various types of artificial intelligence applications. Knowledge engineering focuses on developing intelligent software applications; however, the knowledge embedded in these programs must be sourced from experts, drawing on their extensive experience and insights.

Knowledge acquisition needs to transcend various cognitive and personality obstacles. Extracting the most important insights from the experiences of experts is challenging (Gladwell, 2008), as is persuading them to be receptive to that knowledge. Expert systems are software applications utilized by individuals for educational purposes and making decisions (Milton, 2007).

Strategy of Knowledge Sharing

Knowledge sharing is a generic expression used to designate the *voluntary* transfer of knowledge from one entity to another. A key aspect that sets knowledge sharing apart from general knowledge transfer is the readiness of a specific entity to initiate the process (Antonelli et al., 2008; Davenport & Prusak, 2000; Hislop, 2005; Jashapara, 2011; North & Kumta, 2018).

Entities involved in interorganizational knowledge sharing can include individuals, teams, departments, and even entire organizations. The core process of sharing knowledge involves the social engagement of individuals and their drive to connect with others in communication. A significant result of knowledge sharing is the development of organizational knowledge, which is a fundamental concept in knowledge management.

As noted by Cyr and Choo (2010), the process of knowledge sharing, which is a form of social interaction, entails both costs and benefits. The expenses extend beyond monetary aspects; they also encompass the time and cognitive effort required to convert tacit knowledge into explicit knowledge via externalization. Moreover, the communication process entails a specific effort to standardize information, particularly when the audience consists of individuals with varying abilities to comprehend or absorb the content. There needs to be a harmony between those endeavors and the advantages they provide. In many cases, the benefits of sharing knowledge extend beyond financial gain or tangible rewards. Recognition from peers and acknowledgment in social circles hold greater value than monetary rewards.

Knowledge sharing can be a simple personal experience or a complex strategy designed to enhance organizational learning (Argote, 2013; Örtenblad, 2011; Rhem, 2017). Closely related to knowledge sharing is *knowledge diffusion* (Braunerhjelm et al., 2010; Morone & Taylor, 2004; Shu-hsien Liao, 2003; Valeri & Baggio, 2020c). Knowledge diffusion is a figurative idea drawn from thermodynamics, proposing that the spread of knowledge within a social framework resembles the transfer of heat in a solid material, moving from areas of higher temperature to those of lower temperature. Similarly, understanding regarding a particular field or issue can be disseminated from a person or group possessing greater expertise to a community with less knowledge.

Bratianu (2015) shows that thermodynamics also inspires us to introduce the concept of *knowledge convection*, which implies the motion of people with their embodied knowledge. Knowledge convection is tightly linked to knowledge flow, indicating the interplay between various areas of knowledge within a specific social context. It is intriguing to consider the potential metaphorical concept of knowledge radiation, suggesting a significant disparity between the source and the recipient of a message. That metaphor can be exemplified by the warmth emitted from the Sun to the Earth. When a message goes viral online, it resembles a phenomenon of knowledge spreading, characterized by both its strength and its reach. A solid grasp of knowledge diffusion, knowledge convection, and knowledge radiation can assist managers in becoming more efficient in the intricate process of sharing knowledge.

In the context of organizational knowledge dynamics, it has been suggested by certain authors that knowledge sharing does not lead to the creation of new knowledge. The act of sharing knowledge leads to a general enhancement in the average degree of knowledge within the organization, as well as a transformation in how knowledge is distributed.

Consequently, the organization's knowledge entropy rises, which directly enhances the innovation process with remaining unchanged (Bratianu, 2019). As a result, the strategy for sharing knowledge fosters an environment that encourages innovation and enhances the overall organization's ability to absorb knowledge, keeping as it is. The success of sharing knowledge relies not just on the knowledge level of the sender but also on the recipient's understanding. This suggests that to improve understanding, knowledge sharing should occasionally be accompanied by training initiatives (Reinholdt et al., 2011).

Strategy of Knowledge Exploration

Knowledge exploration aims to assist managers in establishing an environment conducive to the generation of knowledge aligned with key trends in science, technology, economics, business, and consumer behavior.

From this viewpoint, knowledge might already be present within the organization, albeit in various arrangements and forms. Exploring new alternatives of knowledge structuring by using *lateral thinking* (De Bono, 1970), managers may find new solutions to their problems or stimulate incremental innovation.

The approach to knowledge exploration also pertains to the process of knowledge generation at the individual, group, and organizational tiers. In the realm of knowledge management philosophy, the generation of knowledge comes from the transformation of information, which serves as processed data. It is a structured procedure integrated within the data, information, knowledge, and wisdom (DIKW) framework (Davenport & Prusak, 2000; Jashapara, 2011; Liew, 2013; Rowley, 2007).

The DIKW framework is founded on a linear logic structure; however, the relationships among data, information, knowledge, and wisdom are nonlinear. As a result, it is impossible for anyone to clarify the transitions between these elements. The DIKW framework still serves as a model for the layered complexity involved in knowledge processing, but it does not account for how that knowledge is generated.

Bratianu (2015) defined knowledge dynamics as an ongoing interplay among rational, emotional, and spiritual domains. Knowledge creation can occur through the conversion of one type of knowledge into another or through the reorganization of rational understanding, driven by the sharing of knowledge among various cognitive agents.

By engaging in social interactions, personal knowledge is enhanced and converted into organizational knowledge. Consequently, the generation of knowledge emerges from our activities as fresh information. The sensory system processes that data into emotional insights and understanding, facilitated by the cognitive unconscious. By blending the realms of rationality and emotion, emotional understanding is converted into rational insight through the process of reflection. Ultimately, over time, both emotional and rational understanding play a role in the development of spiritual knowledge (Damasio, 1999, 2003, 2012; Fauconnier & Turner, 2002; Friedenberg & Silverman, 2016; LeDoux, 1999; Robinson et al., 2013).

4.5 Knowledge Leader in a Changing Organizational Environment

The new idea of organization as an open system and as a formal system of relations helps to focus the analysis on the conditions of its equilibrium, which can be ensured through the coordination and harmonization of the various subunits that make it up. This equilibrium is not an intrinsic condition of the organization, but it is a characteristic that needs to be maintained and harmonized, through the integrating function typical of the company management level (Sherif, 2006; Valeri, 2021).

This function of integrating the various components of the system ensures that they have a mutual relationship consistent with the general objectives of the system, preventing the development of imbalances potentially able to compromise the correct functioning of the organization.

As we will see, Barnard outlines this function of integration as a real function of the firm's management team, which includes a personal component, leadership, and an impersonal component (Barnard, 1938). While the impersonal functions are mostly aimed at the formal structuring of the organization and the guarantee of its smooth functioning, leadership focuses on the "more human" aspect of the organization, acting as the motivating and supportive element that can significantly influence its success.

Leadership therefore appears as a capacity for aggregation of the various forces within the system, which are encouraged in view of a general and common goal.

Therefore, particularly in today's world, the study of leadership and its attributes is highly significant in the field of business organization, as they are viewed as crucial factors in determining an organization's success or failure.

Leadership is a fundamental component to ensure the solidity and coherence of the system, and this is becoming more and more important if we consider the changed theoretical paradigm that considers the organization as an open system based on the principle of cooperation (Grabo & van Vugt, 2016; Heinz et al., 2006; Zirkler et al., 2022).

Leadership skills can develop according to some main *directives*, which identify as many approaches to the subject. While some theories focus on the primacy recognized to the personal factor and therefore to the personal characteristics that a leader should have, others adopt an approach that focuses on environmental factors and situational variables (Garzia, 2011; Xu & Cooper Thomas, 2011). The results of implementing these approaches have led to the development of theories that in some way combine the influence of environmental factors with the leader's personal characteristics (Valeri, 2021).

At first, attention is focused on the leader's *person*, conceived as an individual with skills and abilities above the average, able to exercise authority, control, and respect over his subordinates. This perspective reveals its shortcomings as it fails to sufficiently consider the influence of context and the surrounding environment on the actual behavior of the leader. Focus initially transitions to the actions involved (such as differentiating between an authoritarian, coercive leadership approach, and a democratic, participatory one) and subsequently to the contextual environmental elements.

The necessity to expand the analysis beyond merely the attribute of personality arises, in part, from the same impetus that drives the transition from viewing an organization as a closed system to perceiving it as an open system (Bhatti et al., 2012; Bowers et al., 2012; Bui et al., 2017; Busse et al., 2018; Davison & Smothers, 2015).

In this scenario, we can recognize the significance of the various ways that environmental factors impact the operations of the organization. It is no longer seen as an isolated entity but rather as a system that is constantly interacting with its surrounding environment, both affecting it and being affected in return.

By adopting this situational approach, it comes out that leadership develops with certain features depending on the conditions in which the organization is and on the values and behavior of its members.

Its effectiveness is associated with its capacity to promote the improvement of the factors that contribute to the organization's success, including the efficient discovery of resources and the accomplishment of shared goals. In every organization, these factors appear uniquely, making it essential to adapt leadership styles to the varying contexts in which they must be applied.

In summary, the effectiveness of various leadership styles depends on the specific situations and contexts. A hallmark of the situational approach is its focus on the *follower* in the context of leadership dynamics.

Thus, it is essential to emphasize that an individual is recognized as a leader because the organization's members acknowledge him as one. As soon as the leadership potential is acknowledged, individuals will naturally feel motivated and inclined to gain his approval, leading to an enhancement in their performance.

Another feature of the situational approach is that different management styles are outlined according to the organizational *challenges* the organization has to face.

An example is provided by the transformational leadership theory, which mainly deals with the capabilities of leadership units in implementing the change. When structural change or renewal of production methods is required, it is essential for management functions to consider not just organizational adjustments but also, and most importantly, the engagement of individuals in the process of change. This approach is crucial for achieving a strong consensus on intentions and goals.

In addition, during transition, a leader must also prove to be capable of maintaining the employees' confidence, clearly explaining what the consequences of the change are and, above all, what the related benefits will be for the members of the organization. Only through a *transformational leadership style* it will be possible to lead an organization into the complex contemporary world, characterized by daily challenges and, above all, by an urgent need to adapt to the rapid and relentless technological development.

As stated above, it is possible to follow a sort of evolutionary line in leadership theories.

Starting from a restricted approach, based only on the leader's personal characteristics, considered as an individual with "superior" skills, the focus shifts toward a more careful vision of the relationship between the leader and the members of the group, by recognizing the increasing importance of all those environmental and external factors that can influence the skills and characteristics of the leadership exercise. As we have seen, the progressive evolution of the concept of leadership follows the evolution of the concept of organization, with a growing centrality of the concept of cooperation and integration.

We are therefore witnessing the transition from a vision of leadership based on the concept of hierarchy and authority, suitable for the rational and scientific conception of business proposed by the classical school, to forms of leadership that aim at favoring participatory and integrated methods in a perspective of a progressive business integration (Valeri, 2021).

According to situational theories, which recommend that leaders and managers adjust to diverse environmental conditions, the significance of the leader as an individual tends to diminish, giving way to the consideration of situational factors. This inconsistency gives rise to theories that aim to merge the "personal" perspective with the situational one, in an effort to balance out the extremes that could result from their unoriginal application (Valeri, 2021).

The main goal of this evolutionary line can be considered the theory of the so-called transformational leadership that considers the environmental situation relevant but, at the same time, states that it can be influenced and even changed by the leader (Ackoff, 1999; Bass, 1999; Bass & Riggio, 2006). In today's rapidly evolving environment, the need for this kind of leadership is increasingly vital as the world undergoes constant change.

Enhancing a Knowledge Culture by a Knowledge Leadership

Knowledge creation and dissemination are significantly influenced by organizational culture. Learning organizations enhance the development journey of every employee by consistently evolving (Aramburu et al., 2015; Prystupa-Rządca, 2017).

Hence, the craving for knowledge serves as a driving force behind the pursuit of learning. Since learning consistently alters our understanding of various aspects, leaders ought to foster an organizational culture that emphasizes knowledge, learning, and innovation both at the individual level and across the organization. This approach should promote the continual transformation of tacit knowledge into explicit knowledge (Kucharska, 2021).

Attaining this is more straightforward when owners articulate their expectations through the organization's vision and business policies supporting the competitive advantage. These expectations are facilitated by a suitable organizational culture (Štrukelj et al., 2020). According to Oliver and Kandadi (2006), it is essential for organizations to have a clear understanding of their culture prior to implementing a knowledge initiative. Numerous other writers endorse this idea, suggesting that organizational culture ought to be the central focus of knowledge management initiatives.

According to Islam et al. (2015), knowledge culture is an environment that encourages the dissemination of knowledge within the organization.

Kucharska (2021) argues that a learning-oriented organization needs to collect, share, and utilize knowledge, allowing its members to work together efficiently in adjusting the organization's reactions to challenges. Learning should take place and be promoted within teams and larger groups, enabling individuals to collectively create new knowledge (Prystupa-Rządca, 2017).

Kucharska and Bedford (2020) observed that the culture of knowledge has a major impact on learning. Creating a knowledge-centric culture demands that management concentrate on three key aspects: readying the organization, overseeing knowledge resources, and utilizing knowledge to gain a competitive edge. Consequently, the authors conclude that the initial phase in fostering a knowledge culture within an organization is to prepare the enterprise, which frequently entails transforming its culture as well as altering how employees collaborate and communicate (Kucharska & Bedford, 2020).

According to Wei and Miraglia (2017), organizational culture plays a significant role in shaping behaviors that are fundamental to knowledge management. Specifically:

1. Culture defines beliefs regarding the nature of knowledge and, consequently, identifies which types of knowledge are valuable for management.
2. Culture influences the interactions between individual knowledge and organizational knowledge.
3. Culture establishes the environment for social interactions, which ultimately dictates the effectiveness of an organization in creating, sharing, and utilizing knowledge, as well as its ability to manage those processes effectively.

Additionally, the knowledge culture within an organization can influence employees' favorable perspectives on both tacit and explicit knowledge, facilitating the seamless progression of all knowledge-related processes (Leone & Schiavone, 2019). Nonetheless, certain organizations have demonstrated greater success in their knowledge management initiatives than others, frequently attributing their achievements to their underlying organizational culture (Oliver & Kandadi, 2006).

As stated by Tennakoon et al. (2022), a significant connection exists between organizational culture and knowledge management. Understanding the cultural context is essential for effectively analyzing and utilizing knowledge.

According to Prystupa-Rządca (2017) and Stylianou and Savva (2016), organizational culture plays a crucial role in two key aspects of knowledge management: the willingness to collaborate and the level of trust among employees.

Knowledge sharing requires active human participation, the interchange of thoughts, and a readiness to be receptive.

The complex dynamics of the present business environment require a new approach to leadership. This approach should focus on collaboratively generating substantial value for all parties involved, not only shareholders but also customers, employees, partners, and the broader community.

Leaders are pivotal in determining whether their organizations succeed or fail. Leaders have the potential to successfully drive change, enhance their organization's abilities, and boost overall performance, or conversely they may fail to do so (Amiri et al., 2020).

The influence of leadership on the governance and management of businesses and enterprises has been acknowledged as a crucial element that can affect an enterprise's performance (Imam & Zaheer, 2021). An appropriate leadership approach has a beneficial effect on the execution of knowledge management in organizations (Islam & Asad, 2021).

According to Amiri et al. (2020), leaders play multiple roles in enhancing an organization's abilities and executing strategic transformations. Leadership empowers executive teams to work together efficiently to instigate change and implement strategies, cultivate processes (Maheshwari & Yadav, 2019), foster skills and mindsets (Allio, 2019), and provide tools necessary for jointly navigating transformations. This approach encourages creativity across the entire organization, manages talent effectively, and fosters a supportive culture (Al-Ghazali, 2020; Longenecker & Insch, 2018).

As noted by Maheshwari and Yadav (2019), leadership and the growth of enterprises are interconnected aspects of a single process aimed at boosting the capabilities of businesses and individuals to enhance their effectiveness.

In terms of knowledge leadership, there is evidence suggesting that knowledge-focused leadership positively influences knowledge management (Donate & De Pablo, 2015; Jad et al., 2017; Sadeghi & Rad, 2018), as well as contributes positively to the processes of knowledge creation and application (Safari & Azadehdel, 2015).

Leaders confront swift transformations prompted by emerging technologies, globalization, political dynamics (Yi, 2019), and environmental issues. They reshape the fundamental values, beliefs, and attitudes of their followers to enhance the organization's ability to foster positive change (Amiri et al., 2020). Leaders hold a vital position of power within their organizations (Maheshwari & Yadav, 2019).

Knowledge leadership is becoming increasingly acknowledged as a crucial factor for organizations aiming to improve their knowledge management practices (Yanga et al., 2014). Additionally, knowledge management has been advocated as a method to improve the performance of enterprises.

When organizations are considered as learning systems, the leader's role can facilitate guidance in the learning journey (Kragt & Guenter, 2018). The functions of leaders within a learning organization have been identified as coaches, facilitators, educators, learning leaders, and developers (Allio, 2019). Unlike knowledge management, knowledge leadership involves the ongoing enhancement and innovation of information resources, personal competencies, and networks for knowledge and learning (Berraies & Chouiref, 2023; Fischer et al., 2021).

Knowledge leadership refers to a process in which one person aids other members of a group in the necessary learning activities aimed at achieving the objectives of the group or organization (Berraies, 2020; Steinerowska-Streb & Wziątek-Staśko, 2020; Yin et al., 2020). In addition, knowledge leadership can aid in creating systems for accountability and control, along with facilitating the sharing of customer knowledge (Goswami & Agrawal, 2021). Furthermore, strong knowledge leadership can enhance the effective integration, sharing, and management of customer knowledge (Imam & Zaheer, 2021). A knowledge leader acts as a driving force for fostering a culture of knowledge sharing and is responsible for the specifications of the infrastructure that enables the transfer and storage of customer knowledge and oversees the maintenance of a closed-loop learning system.

4.6 Knowledge Management and Competitive Advantage

Knowledge management involves recognizing and outlining the essential knowledge resources, beginning with defining the key competencies needed to oversee the business and its operations, as well as assessing the condition of the present knowledge assets.

In this context, knowledge management is viewed as the oversight of the strategic, technological, and cultural elements involved in the processes of acquiring, storing, sharing, and validating knowledge that is deemed essential for the organization's success and competitive edge. This approach emphasizes the learning aspect and enhances the organizational facet through the implementation of advanced technologies.

Consequently, KM is essentially a management function and must be aligned with the organization's strategies and business goals. Knowledge management initiatives should be implemented with the goal of addressing business challenges and enhancing the organization's performance, rather than simply focusing on knowledge management as an objective on its own (Mills & Smith, 2011; Muthuveloo et al., 2017; Zack et al., 2009).

In this regard, Forcadell and Guadamillas (2002) defined knowledge management as the organization and modification of systems, simple tools, and mechanisms that support the thorough oversight of knowledge throughout different sectors and hierarchical levels within an organization, ultimately promoting changes in products and workflows.

Organizations can achieve a competitive edge by recruiting, nurturing, and retaining individuals who demonstrate a talent for acquiring and retaining information, as well as a proficiency in improving and honing their collective knowledge resources.

In alignment with the aforementioned points, managerial staff will have the potential to convert the organization into a body that possesses the desire, capacity, and proficiency to secure a competitive advantage in the marketplace, aided by knowledge (Ichijo & Kohlbacher, 2007).

For knowledge to be beneficial, it must be continually updated through consistent and ongoing efforts to preserve its relevance. Once knowledge is generated, it must be safeguarded against theft, as this will help the organization maintain its competitive advantage in the market (Wensley et al., 2011). The approach should focus on the acquisition and preservation of knowledge that remains perpetually valuable, allowing the organization to leverage it for achieving a competitive edge. This principle must be integrated into the organization's core competencies (Ichijo & Nonaka, 2006).

An organization that invests time in creating and implementing an effective knowledge management system achieves a competitive advantage by obtaining essential decision-making information in seconds and circumventing the significant costs related to delays. Knowledge management systems function as a lasting "collective intelligence" repository for the memories and records of an organization, contributed by both present and former employees.

This system is utilized to sharpen the organization's competitive advantage by maintaining the currency and relevance of knowledge while keeping as it is.

Efficient knowledge management provides a competitive edge by facilitating better-informed decision-making (Inkpen & Tsang, 2005). Firms enhance their competitive edge by leveraging knowledge management systems to strengthen their essential capabilities, which are vital for effective business functions. Utilizing the accumulated knowledge, a comprehensive understanding of customer and market conditions is created, allowing employees to see a "framework" that they can later enhance by leveraging the available knowledge resources, resulting in increased productivity and efficiency (Sanchez & Heene, 1997).

To ensure operational competitiveness, an organization must foster a collaborative and trustworthy community, where members have confidence in one another, which facilitates more effective and efficient sharing and documentation of knowledge (Bramwell & Lane, 2000). To establish trust, it is essential to develop an effective knowledge management system that provides the necessary knowledge resources whenever needed.

According to Wickramasinghe (2003), knowledge management plays an essential role in tackling significant challenges faced by organizations, including the necessity to innovate and stay competitive. A competitive advantage refers to the capacity to achieve higher profits than the average in the industry. There are various methods to establish a lasting competitive edge, such as benefiting from economies of scale, obtaining resources, leveraging size (Ghemawat, 1986; Porter, 1985), and sometimes sheer luck. Leveraging knowledge management can enhance the operations of the organization and boost the worth of its resources, thereby making it harder for rivals to replicate (Barney, 1986). Consequently, this suggests that it is important to implement knowledge management efficiently.

References

Ackoff, R. L. (1999). Transformational leadership. *Strategy & Leadership, 27*(1), 20–25. https://doi.org/10.1108/eb054626

Al-Ghazali, B. M. (2020). Transformational leadership, career adaptability, job embeddedness and perceived career success: A serial mediation model. *Leadership & Organization Development Journal, 41*(8), 993–1013.

Aljuwaiber, A. (2016). Communities of practice as an initiative for knowledge sharing in business organisations: A literature review. *Journal of Knowledge Management, 20*(4), 731–748. https://doi.org/10.1108/JKM-12-2015-0494

Allio, R. J. (2019). Becoming a leader—First, take charge of your own learning process. *Strategy & Leadership, 46*(3), 21–28.

Amiri, N. A. I., Eladwiah, R., Rahim, A., & Ahmed, G. (2020). Leadership styles and organizational knowledge management activities: A systematic review Gadjah Mada. *International Journal of Business, 22*(3), 250–275.

Andriessen, D. (2004). *Making sense of intellectual capital: Designing a method for the valuation of intangibles*. Elsevier.

Andriopoulos, C., & Lewis, M. (2009). Exploitation-exploration tensions and organizational ambidexterity: Managing paradoxes of innovation. *Organization Science, 20*(4), 696–717.

Antonelli, G., Mollona, E., & Moschera, L. (2008). Burt-or Coleman-type rents, or a bit of both? Knowledge management strategies in suppliers's networks. *International Journal of Business and Management, 13*(12), 274–290. https://doi.org/10.5539/ijbm.v13n12p274

Antonelli, G. (2013). The local innovation networks: An explorative study of success cluster. *The Business Review, 21*(2), 205.

Aramburu, N., Saenz, J., & Blanco, C. (2015). Structural capital, innovation capability, and company performance in technology-based Colombian firms. *Cuadernos de Gestion, 15*(1), 39–60.

Argote, L. (2013). *Organizational learning: Creating, retaining and transferring knowledge* (2nd ed.). Springer.

Argyris, C., & Schon, D. (1978). *Organizational learning: A theory of action perspective*. Addison-Wesley.

Awad, E. M. (2007). *Knowledge management*. Pearson Education India.

Baggio, R., & Valeri, M. (2020). Network science and sustainable performance of family businesses in tourism. *Journal of Family Business Management, 12*, 200. https://doi.org/10.1108/JFBM-06-2020-0048

Barnard, C. (1938). *The functions of the executive*. Harvard University Press.

Barney, J. B. (1986). Organizational culture: Can it be a source of sustained competitive advantage? *Academy of Management Review, 11*(3), 656–665.

Bass, B. M. (1999). Two decades of research and development in transformational leadership. *European Journal of Work and Organizational Psychology, 8*(1), 9–32. https://doi.org/10.1080/135943299398410

Bass, B. M., & Riggio, R. E. (2006). *Transformational leadership* (2nd ed.). Psychology Press. https://doi.org/10.4324/9781410617095

Berraies, S. (2020). Effect of middle managers' cultural intelligence on firms' innovation performance: Knowledge sharing as mediator and collaborative climate as moderator. *Personnel Review, 49*(4), 1015–1038.

Berraies, S., & Chouiref, A. (2023). Exploring the effect of team climate on knowledge management in teams through team work engagement: Evidence from knowledge-intensive firms. *Journal of Knowledge Management, 27*(3), 842–869. https://doi.org/10.1108/JKM-09-2021-0720

Bhatt, G. D. (2001). Knowledge management in organizations: Examining the interaction between technologies, techniques, and people. *Journal of Knowledge Management, 5*(1), 68–75. https://doi.org/10.1108/13673270110384419

Bhatti, N., Maitlo, G. M., Shaikh, N., Hashmi, M. A., & Shaikh, F. M. (2012). The impact of autocratic and democratic leadership style on job satisfaction. *International Business Research, 5*, 192.

Böhme, G., & Stehr, N. (Eds.). (1986). *The knowledge society: The growing impact of scientific knowledge in social relations*. D. Reidel Publishing.

Bolisani, E., & Bratianu, C. (2018). *Emergent knowledge strategies: Strategic thinking in knowledge management*. Springer.

Bolisani, E., & Scarso, E. (2014). The place of communities of practice in knowledge management studies: A critical review. *Journal of Knowledge Management, 18*(2), 366–381. https://doi.org/10.1108/JKM-07-2013-0277

Bowers, K. W., Robertson, M., & Parchman, M. L. (2012). How inclusive leadership can help your practice adapt to change: The most effective leaders realize that everyone's input is valuable. *Family Practice Management, 19*(1), 8–26.

Bramwell, B., & Lane, B. (2000). *Tourism collaboration and partnerships: Politics practice and sustainability*. Channel View Publications.

Bratianu, C. (2011). Changing paradigm for knowledge metaphors from dynamics to thermodynamics. *Systems Research and Behavioral Science, 28*(2), 160–169.

Bratianu, C. (2013). Nonlinear integrators of the organizational intellectual capital. In M. Fathi (Ed.), *Integration of practice-oriented knowledge technology: Trends and perspectives* (pp. 3–16). Springer.

Bratianu, C. (2015). *Organizational knowledge dynamics: Managing knowledge creation, acquisition, sharing, and transformation*. IGI Global.

Bratianu, C. (2019). Exploring knowledge entropy in organizations. *Management Dynamics in the Knowledge Economy, 7*(3), 353–366.

Bratianu, C. (2022). *Knowledge strategies*. Cambridge University Press.

Braunerhjelm, P., Acs, Z. J., Audredtsch, D., & Carlsson, B. (2010). The missing link: Knowledge diffusion and entrepreneurship in endogenous growth. *Small Business Economics, 34*(2), 105–125.

Brown, J. S., & Duguid, P. (1991). Organizational learning and communities of practice: Toward a unified view of working, learning, and innovation. *Organizational Science, 2*(1), 40–57.

Brown, J. S., & Duguid, P. (1998). Organizing knowledge. *California Management Review, 40*(3), 90–111.

Bui, H. T., Zeng, Y., & Higgs, M. (2017). The role of person-job fit in the relationship between transformational leadership and job engagement. *Journal of Managerial Psychology, 32*, 373–386.

Busse, R., Kwon, S., Kloep, H. A., Ghosh, K., & Warner, M. (2018). Toward a "meaningful self" at the workplace: Multinational evidence from Asia, Europe, and North America. *Journal of Leadership & Organizational Studies, 25*, 63–75.

Cameron, K. S., & Quinn, R. E. (2011). *Diagnosing and changing organizational culture: Based on the competing values framework* (3rd ed.). Jossey-Bass.

Chan, I., & Chao, C. K. (2008). Knowledge management in small and medium-sized enterprises. *Communications of the ACM, 51*(4), 83–88.

Chaston, I., & Mangles, T. (2000). Business networks: Assisting knowledge management and competence acquisition within UK manufacturing firms. *Journal of Small Business and Enterprise Development, 7*(2), 160–170.

Clark, R. E., Feldon, D. F., van Merrieboer, J. J. G., Yates, K. A., & Early, S. (2008). Cognitive task analysis. In J. M. Spector & M. D. Driscall (Eds.), *Handbook of research on educational communications and technology* (3rd ed., pp. 578–593). Taylor & Francis.

Collis, D. (1996). Organizational capability as a source of profit. In B. Moingeon & A. Edmondson (Eds.), *Organizational learning and competitive advantage*. Sage.

Cyr, S., & Choo, C. W. (2010). The individual and social dynamics of knowledge sharing: An exploratory study. *The Journal of Documentation, 66*(6), 824–846.

Daft, R. L., & Weick, K. E. (1984). Toward a model of organizations as interpretation systems. *Academy of Management Review, 9*, 284–295.

Dalkir, K. (2005). *Knowledge management in theory and practice*. Elsevier.

Damasio, A. R. (1999). *The feelings of what happens: Body and emotion in making of conscious*. Harcourt.

Damasio, A. R. (2003). *Looking for Spinoza: Joy, sorrow, and the feeling brain*. Harcourt.

Damasio, A. R. (2012). *Self comes to mind: Constructing the conscious brain*. Vintage Book.

Darroch, J. (2003). Developing a measure of knowledge management behaviors and practices. *Journal of Knowledge Management, 7*(5), 41–54. https://doi.org/10.1108/13673270310505377

Davenport, E., & Hall, H. (2002). Organizational knowledge and communities of practice. *Annual Review of Information Science and Technology, 36*(1), 170–227. https://doi.org/10.1002/aris.1440360105

Davenport, T. H., & Prusak, L. (2000). *Working knowledge: How organizations manage what they know*. Harvard Business School Press.

Davison, H. K., & Smothers, J. (2015). How theory X style of management arose from a fundamental attribution error. *Journal of Management History, 21*, 210–231.

De Bono, E. (1970). *Lateral thinking: Creativity step by step*. Harper & Row.

Donate, M. J., & De Pablo, J. D. S. (2015). The role of knowledge-oriented leadership in knowledge management practices and innovation. *Journal of Business Research, 68*, 360–370.

Drucker, P. (1993). *Innovation and entrepreneurship: Practice and principles*. Harper Collins Publishers.

Durst, S., & Edvardson, I. R. (2012). Knowledge management in SMEs: A literature review. *Journal of Knowledge Management, 16*(6), 879–903.

Edvinsson, L. (2002). *Corporate longitude: What you need to know to navigate the knowledge economy*. Prentice Hall.

Eucker, T. R. (2007). Understanding the impact of tacit knowledge loss. *Knowledge Management Review, 10*(2), 10–13.

Fauconnier, G., & Turner, M. (2002). *The way we think: Conceptual blending and the mind's hidden complexities*. Basic Books.

Fiol, C. M., & Lyles, M. A. (1985). Organizational learning. *Academy of Management Review, 10*, 803–813.

Fischer, B., Salles-Filho, S., Zeitoum, C., & Colugnati, F. (2021). Performance drivers in knowledge intensive entrepreneurial firms: A multidimensional perspective. *Journal of Knowledge Management, 26*(5), 1–17.

Fletcher, M., & Harris, S. (2012). Knowledge acquisition for the internationalization of the smaller firm: Content and sources. *International Business Review, 21*(4), 631–647.

Forcadell, F. J., & Guadamillas, F. (2002). A case study on the implementation of a knowledge management strategy oriented to innovation. *Knowledge and Process Management, 9*(3), 162–171.

Friedenberg, J., & Silverman, G. (2016). *Cognitive science: An introduction to the study of mind* (3rd ed.). SAGE.

Fugate, B. S., Stank, T. P., & Mentzer, J. T. (2009). Linking improved knowledge management to operational and organizational performance. *Journal of Operations Management, 27*(3), 247–264. https://doi.org/10.1016/j.jom.2008.09.003

Garavelli, C., Gorgoglione, M., & Scozzi, B. (2004). Knowledge management strategy and organization: A perspective of analysis. *Knowledge and Process Management, 11*, 273–282. https://doi.org/10.1002/kpm.209

Garzia, D. (2011). The personalization of politics in Western democracies: Causes and consequences on leader–follower relationships. *The Leadership Quarterly, 22*(4), 697–709. https://doi.org/10.1016/j.leaqua.2011.05.010

Ghemawat, P. (1986). Sustainable advantage. *Harvard Business Review, 64*(5), 53–58.

Gladwell, M. (2008). *Outliers: The story of success*. Penguin Books.

Gold, A. H., Malhotra, A., & Segars, A. H. (2001). Knowledge management: An organizational capabilities perspective. *Journal of Management Information Systems, 18*(1), 185–214. https://doi.org/10.1080/07421222.2001.11045669

Goswami, A. K., & Agrawal, R. K. (2021). Does ethical leadership and psychological capital promote knowledge creation? An empirical study of research organizations. *VINE Journal of Information and Knowledge Management Systems, 53*(6), 1307–1331. https://doi.org/10.1108/VJIKMS-07-2021-0113

Grabo, A., & van Vugt, M. (2016). Charismatic leadership and the evolution of cooperation. *Evolution and Human Behavior, 37*(5), 399–406. https://doi.org/10.1016/j.evolhumbehav.2016.03.005

Grant, R. (1996). Towards a knowledge-based theory of the firm. *Strategic Management Journal, 17*(Special Issue), 109–122.

Gruber, T. R. (1989). Automated knowledge acquisition for strategic knowledge. *Machine Learning, 4*, 293–336. https://doi.org/10.1007/BF00130716

Heinz, U., Baga, T., Gebert, D., & Kearney, E. (2006). Leadership and cooperation as success factors in innovative R&D projects on electronic platforms. *Team Performance Management, 12*(3/4), 66–76. https://doi.org/10.1108/13527590610674077

Hislop, D. (2005). *Knowledge management in organizations: A critical introduction*. Oxford University Press.

Hoe, S. L., & McShane, S. (2010). Structural and informal knowledge acquisition and dissemination in organizational learning: An exploratory analysis. *The Learning Organization, 17*(4), 364–386.

Huber, G. P. (1991). Organizational learning: The contributing processes and the literature. *Organizational Science, 2*(1), 88–115.

Ichijo, K., & Kohlbacher, F. (2007). The Toyota way of global knowledge creation the 'learn local, act global' strategy. *International Journal of Automotive Technology and Management, 7*(2–3), 116–134.

Ichijo, K., & Nonaka, I. (2006). *Knowledge creation and management: New challenges for managers*. Oxford University Press.

Imam, H., & Zaheer, M. K. (2021). Shared leadership and project success: The roles of knowledge sharing, cohesion and trust in the team. *International Journal of Project Management, 39*(5), 463–473.

Immordino-Yang, M. H., Darling-Hammond, L., & Krone, C. R. (2019). Nurturing nature: How brain development is inherently social and emotional, and what this means for education. *Educational Psychologist, 54*(3), 185–204. https://doi.org/10.1080/00461520.2019.1633924

Inkpen, A. C., & Tsang, E. W. K. (2005). Social capital, networks, and knowledge transfer. *Academy of Management Review, 30*(1), 146.

Innocenti, N., & Lazzeretti, L. (2019). Growth in regions, knowledge bases and relatedness: Some insights from the Italian case. *European Planning Studies*, 1–15., ISSN: 0965-4313. https://doi.org/10.1080/09654313.2019.1588862

Islam, T., & Asad, M. (2021). Enhancing employees' creativity through entrepreneurial leadership: Can knowledge sharing and creative self-efficacy matter? *VINE Journal of Information and Knowledge Management Systems, 54*, 59. https://doi.org/10.1108/VJIKMS-07-2021-0121

Islam, M. Z., Jasimuddin, S. M., & Hasan, I. (2015). Organizational culture, structure, technology infrastructure and knowledge sharing. *VINE Journal of Information and Knowledge Management Systems, 45*(1), 67–88.

Jackson, M. C. (2019). *Critical systems thinking and the management of complexity*. John Wiley & Sons.

Jad, S. M. M., Geravandi, S., Mohammadi, M. J., Alizadeh, R., Sarvarian, M., Rastegarimeh, B., Afkar, A., & Mohammad, H. (2017). *The relationship between knowledge of leadership and knowledge management practices in the food industry in Kurdistan province*. https://doi.org/10.1016/j.dib.2019.103995

Janis, I. L., & Mann, L. (1977). *Decision-making: A psychological analysis of conflict, choice, and commitment*. The Free Press.

Jashapara, A. (2011). *Knowledge management: An integrated approach* (2nd ed.). Financial Times/Prentice Hall.

Kragt, D., & Guenter, H. (2018). Why and when leadership training predicts effectiveness: The role of leader identity and leadership experience. *Leadership & Organization Development Journal, 39*(3), 406–418.

Kucharska, W. (2021). Leadership, culture, intellectual capital and knowledge processes for organizational innovativeness across industries: The case of Poland. *Journal of Intellectual Capital, 22*(7), 121–141.

Kucharska, W., & Bedford, D. A. D. (2020). Love your mistakes!—They help you adapt to change. How do knowledge, collaboration and learning cultures foster organizational intelligence? *Journal of Organizational Change Management, 33*(7), 1329–1354.

Kukami, C., & Armstrong, S. (2009). *The SAGE handbook of management learning, education and development.* SAGE.

Lakoff, G., & Johnson, M. (1999). *Philosophy in the flesh: The embodied mind and its challenge to western thought.* Basic Books.

Lazzeretti, L., Capone, F., Caloffi, A., & Sedita, S. R. (2019). Rethinking clusters. Towards a new research agenda for cluster research. *European Planning Studies, 27*, 1879–1903., ISSN: 0965-4313. https://doi.org/10.1080/09654313.2019.1650899

LeDoux, J. (1999). *The emotional brain: The mysterious underpinnings of emotional life*. Phoenix.

Leone, D., & Schiavone, F. (2019). Innovation and knowledge sharing in crowdfunding: How social dynamics affect project success. *Technology Analysis and Strategic Management, 31*(7), 803–816.

Liao, S. H., Wu, C. C., Hu, D. C., & Tsui, K. A. (2010). Relationships between knowledge acquisition, absorptive capacity and innovation capability: An empirical study on Taiwan's financial and manufacturing industries. *Journal of Information Science, 36*(1), 19–35.

Liew, A. (2013). DIKIW: Data, information, knowledge, intelligence, wisdom and their interrelationships. *Business Management Dynamics, 2*(10), 49–62.

Longenecker, C., & Insch, G. S. (2018). Senior leaders' strategic role in leadership development. *Strategic HR Review, 17*(3), 143–149.

Maheshwari, S. K., & Yadav, J. (2019). The role of HR in leadership development. *Development and Learning in Organizations, 33*(5), 20–23.

March, J. G. (1988). *Decisions and organizations*. Blackwell.

March, J. G. (1991). Exploration and exploitation in organizational learning. *Organization Science, 2*(1), 71–87.

Mills, A. M., & Smith, T. A. (2011). Knowledge management and organizational performance: A decomposed view. *Journal of Knowledge Management, 15*(1), 156–171. https://doi.org/10.1108/13673271111108756

Milton, N. R. (2007). *Knowledge acquisition in practice: A step-by-step guide*. Springer.

Milton, N., Shadbolt, N., Cottam, H., & Hammersley, M. (1999). Towards a knowledge technology for knowledge management. *International Journal of Human-Computer Studies, 51*(3), 615–641. https://doi.org/10.1006/ijhc.1999.0278

Morone, J., & Taylor, R. (2004). Knowledge diffusion dynamics and network properties of face-to-face interactions. *Journal of Evolutionary Economics, 14*(3), 327–351.

Muthuveloo, R., Shanmugam, N., & Teoh, A. P. (2017). The impact of tacit knowledge management on organizational performance: Evidence from Malaysia. *Asia Pacific Management Review, 22*(4), 192–201. https://doi.org/10.1016/j.apmrv.2017.07.010

Nonaka, I., & Takeuchi, H. (1995). *The knowledge—Creating company: How Japanese companies create the dynamics of innovation.* Oxford University Press.

North, K., & Kumta, G. (2018). *Knowledge management: Value creation through organizational learning* (2nd ed.). Springer.

Noruzy, A., Dalfard, V. M., Azhdari, B., Nazari-Shirkouhi, S., & Rezazadeh, A. (2013). Relations between transformational leadership, organizational learning, knowledge management, organizational innovation, and organizational performance: An empirical investigation of manufacturing firms. *International Journal of Advanced Manufacturing Technology, 64*, 1073–1085. https://doi.org/10.1007/s00170-012-4038-y

Oliver, S., & Kandadi, K. R. (2006). How to develop knowledge culture in organizations? A multiple case study of large distributed organizations. *Journal of Knowledge Management, 10*(4), 6–24.

Oluikpe, P. (2012). Developing a corporate knowledge management strategy. *Journal of Knowledge Management, 16*(6), 862–878. https://doi.org/10.1108/13673271211276164

Orr, J. E. (1990). Sharing knowledge, celebrating identity: Community memory in a service culture. In D. Middleton & D. Edwards (Eds.), *Collective remembering*. Sage Publications.

Örtenblad, A. (2011). *Making sense of the learning organization: What is it and who needs it?* Yayasan Ilmuwan.

Pattinson, S., & Preece, D. (2014). Communities of practice, knowledge acquisition and innovation: A case study of science-based SMEs. *Journal of Knowledge Management, 18*(1), 107–120. https://doi.org/10.1108/JKM-05-2013-0168

Pellegrino, J. M., & McNaughton, R. B. (2015). The co-evolution of learning and internationalization strategy in international new ventures. *Management International Review, 55*, 457–483.

Polanyi, M. (1962). *Personal knowledge: Towards a post-critical philosophy*. The University of Chicago Press.

Polanyi, M. (1983). *The tacit dimension*. Peter Smith.

Porter, M. E. (1985). Technology and competitive advantage. *Journal of Business Strategy, 5*, 60.

Prystupa-Rządca, K. (2017). The role of organizational culture in knowledge management in small companies. *Journal of Entrepreneurship, Management and Innovation, 13*(3), 151–173.

Raisch, S., Birkinshaw, J., Probst, G., & Tushman, M. L. (2009). Organizational ambidexterity: Balancing exploitation and exploration for sustained performance. *Organization Science, 20*(4), 685–695.

Reinholdt, M., Pederson, T., & Foss, N. J. (2011). Why a central network position isn't enough: The role of motivation and ability for knowledge sharing in employee networks. *Academy of Management Journal, 54*(6), 1277–1299.

Rhem, A. J. (2017). *Knowledge management in practice*. CRC Press.

Ricceri, F. (2008). *Intellectual capital and knowledge management. Strategic management of knowledge resources*. Routledge.

Robinson, M. D., Watkins, E. R., & Harmon-Jones, E. (Eds.). (2013). *Handbook of cognition and emotion*. The Guilford Press.

Rowley, J. (2007). The wisdom hierarchy: Representations of DIKW hierarchy. *Journal of Information Science, 33*(2), 163–180.

Russell, B. (2009). *Human knowledge: Its scope and limits*. Routledge.

Sadeghi, A., & Rad, F. M. (2018). The role of knowledge-oriented leadership in knowledge management and innovation. *Management Science Letters, 8*, 151–160.

Safari, A., & Azadehdel, M. R. (2015). The key role of knowledge-oriented leadership in innovation performance of manufacturing and commercial companies of Guilan province. *International Letters of Social and Humanistic Sciences, 62*, 1–7.

Sahlin-Andersson, K., & Engwall, L. (Eds.). (2002). *The expansion of management knowledge. Carriers, flows, and sources*. Stanford Business Books.

Sanchez, R., & Heene, A. (1997). A competence perspective on strategic learning and knowledge management. In R. Sanchez & A. Heene (Eds.), *Strategic learning and knowledge management* (pp. 3–18). Wiley.

Savage, C. M. (1990). *5th generation management*. Butterworth-Heinemann.

Sherif, K. (2006). An adaptive strategy for managing knowledge in organizations. *Journal of Knowledge Management, 10*(4), 72–80. https://doi.org/10.1108/13673270610679372

Shu-hsien Liao, S. H. (2003). Knowledge management technologies and applications—Literature review from 1995 to 2002. *Expert Systems with Applications, 25*(2), 155–164. https://doi.org/10.1016/S0957-4174(03)00043-5

Simon, H. A. (1976). *Administrative behavior: A study of decision-making processes in administrative organizations* (3rd ed.). The Free Press.

Spender, J.-C. (1996). Making knowledge the basis of a dynamic theory of the firm. *Strategic Management Journal, 17*(Special Issue), 45–62.

Steinerowska-Streb, I., & Wziątek-Staśko, A. (2020). Innovations in family firms: A study of owner-managers' knowledge development. *Journal of Family Business Management, 10*(3), 247–264.

Štrukelj, T., Nikolić, J., Zlatanović, D., & Sternad ZabukovŠek, S. (2020). A strategic model for sustainable business policy development. *Sustainability, 12*(2), 1–28.

Stylianou, V., & Savva, A. (2016). Investigating the knowledge management culture. *Universal Journal of Educational Research, 4*(7), 1515–1521.

Sveiby, K. E. (2001). A knowledge-based theory of the firm to guide in strategy formulation. *Journal of Intellectual Capital, 2*(4), 344–358.

Tennakoon, T. M. M. P., Kulatunga, U., & Jayasena, H. S. (2022). Influence of organisational culture on knowledge management in BIM-enabled construction environments. *VINE Journal of Information and Knowledge Management Systems, 52*(2), 224–242.

Valeri, M. (2016). Networking and cooperation practices in the Italian tourism business. *Journal of Tourism, Heritage & Services Marketing, 2*(1), 30–35. http://doi.org/10.5281/zenodo.376333

Valeri, M. (2021). *Tourism risk. Crisis and recovery management*. Emerald Publishing.

Valeri, M., & Baggio, R. (2020a). Social network analysis: Organizational implications in tourism management. *International Journal of Organizational Analysis, 29*, 342. https://doi.org/10.1108/IJOA-12-2019-1971

Valeri, M., & Baggio, R. (2020b). Italian tourism intermediaries: A social network analysis exploration. *Current Issues in Tourism, 24*(9), 1270–1283. https://doi.org/10.1080/13683500.2020.1777950

Valeri, M., & Baggio, R. (2020c). A critical reflection on the adoption of blockchain in tourism. *Journal Information Technology and Tourism, 23*(2), 121–132. https://doi.org/10.1007/s40558-020-00183-1

Valeri, M., & Baggio, R. (2021). Increasing the efficiency of knowledge transfer in Italian tourism system: A network approach. *Current Issues in Tourism, 25*, 2127. https://doi.org/10.1080/13683500.2021.1937960

Wei, Y., & Miraglia, S. (2017). Organizational culture and knowledge transfer in project-based organizations: Theoretical insights from a Chinese construction firm. *International Journal of Project Management, 35*(4), 571–585.

Weick, K. (1979). *The social psychology of organizing*. Random House.

Wenger, E. (1988). *Communities of practice: Learning, meaning, and identity*. Cambridge University Press.

Wenger, E., McDermott, R., & Snyder, W. M. (2002). *A guide to managing knowledge: Cultivating communities of practice*. Harvard Business School Press.

Wensley, A. K. P., Gabriel Cegarra-Navarro, J., Cepeda-Carrión, G., & Genaro Leal Millán, A. (2011). How entrepreneurial actions transform customer capital through time: Exploring and exploiting knowledge in an open-mindedness context. *International Journal of Manpower, 32*(1), 132–150. https://doi.org/10.1108/01437721111121279

Wickramasinghe, N. (2003). Do we practise what we preach? Are knowledge management systems in practice truly reflective of knowledge management systems in theory? *Business Process Management Journal, 9*, 295.

Wielinga, B. J., Schreiber, A. T., & Breuker, J. A. (1992). KADS: A modelling approach to knowledge engineering. *Knowledge Acquisition, 4*(1), 5–53. https://doi.org/10.1016/1042-8143(92)90013-Q

Wiig, K. M. (1997). Knowledge management: Where did it come from and where will it go? *Expert Systems with Applications, 13*(1), 1–14. https://doi.org/10.1016/S0957-4174(97)00018-3

Xu, J., & Cooper Thomas, H. (2011). How can leaders achieve high employee engagement? *Leadership & Organization Development Journal, 32*(4), 399–416. https://doi.org/10.1108/01437731111134661

Yanga, L. R., Huang, C. F., & Hsu, T. J. (2014). Knowledge leadership to improve project and organizational performance. Knowledge leadership to improve project and organizational performance. *International Journal of Project Management, 32*(1), 40–53.

Yi, Z. (2019). A leader's approaches to fostering a culture of knowledge sharing in an information organization. *Library Management, 40*(8/9), 593–600.

Yin, J., Ma, Z., Yu, H., Jia, M., & Liao, G. (2020). Transformational leadership and employee knowledge sharing: Explore the mediating roles of psychological safety and team efficacy. *Journal of Knowledge Management, 24*(2), 150–171.

Zack, M., McKeen, J., & Singh, S. (2009). Knowledge management and organizational performance: An exploratory analysis. *Journal of Knowledge Management, 13*(6), 392–409. https://doi.org/10.1108/13673270910997088

Zirkler, M., Knoepffler, N., & Albrecht, R. (2022). Leadership and cooperation: Ethical considerations and moral frameworking. In V. Schulte, C. Steinebach, & K. Veth (Eds.), *Mindful leadership in practice*. Springer. https://doi.org/10.1007/978-3-030-97311-7_12

5 AI and Knowledge Management in Modern Organizations

5.1 Maintaining Knowledge Quality

The most enduring challenge is the problem of isolated knowledge compartments. Knowledge silos arise when information and expertise remain restricted to departments or teams instead of being disseminated throughout the organization. These silos can result in inefficiencies, as various sectors within the organization might replicate efforts or overlook important insights that could enhance decision-making and foster innovation (Biswas et al., 2024; Jassawalla & Sashittal, 2002; Spectre, 2019).

The underlying reason for knowledge silos frequently stems from organizational frameworks that emphasize departmental independence rather than fostering cross-functional teamwork, along with cultural elements like insufficient trust or a competitive attitude among staff (Intezari et al., 2017; Ismail Al-Alawi et al., 2007).

To eliminate these silos, it is essential to intentionally foster a culture of knowledge sharing and to establish knowledge management systems that enable the seamless exchange of information across different areas of the organization.

Nonetheless, breaking down knowledge silos continues to be a major obstacle for numerous organizations, especially those that have intricate, layered structures. One significant obstacle in knowledge management is ensuring the quality of information retained within an organization (Khorashaadizadeh et al., 2024).

As information is constantly being generated and disseminated, there exists a possibility that obsolete, incorrect, or unrelated data might build up in knowledge stores, resulting in a decline in the quality of that knowledge.

Subpar knowledge can lead to significant repercussions, such as erroneous decision-making, increased inefficiencies, and a decline in confidence in the KM system. To uphold the quality of knowledge, it is essential to continuously work on updating and organizing knowledge resources, so that only the most precise and pertinent information is preserved. The challenge is heightened by the vast amount

M. Valeri, *Organizations and Knowledge Management*, Knowledge Management and Organizational Learning 16, https://doi.org/10.1007/978-3-031-97954-5_5

of information produced by organizations, which complicates the efficient monitoring and management of all knowledge.

Additionally, the task of upholding the quality of knowledge typically rests with a limited team of knowledge managers or IT staff, which may result in bottlenecks and delays. To tackle this issue, organizations need to create well-defined governance structures for knowledge management, specifying distinct roles and responsibilities for both knowledge curation and quality assurance (Kyoon Yoo et al., 2011; Lim et al., 1999; Zeynep et al., 2008).

Moreover, utilizing technologies like artificial intelligence and machine learning can assist in streamlining the task of recognizing and eliminating outdated or subpar information from knowledge databases. The incorporation of technology poses another major obstacle in the deployment of knowledge management systems.

Although advanced KM technologies have the potential to significantly improve the efficiency and effectiveness of knowledge management, their successful implementation frequently encounters challenges such as user resistance, expenses, and compatibility with present systems. Employees might hesitate to embrace new knowledge management tools because they are unfamiliar with them, find them complicated, or worry about how these tools could affect their workflow. This resistance may be especially noticeable in organizations that have a long-standing reliance on conventional, paper-based methods for managing knowledge (Malhotra, 2005; Schulte & Sample, 2006).

Additionally, the expenses associated with both the implementation and upkeep of advanced KM technologies can be very high, particularly for smaller organizations that operate within tight budget constraints.

Moreover, incorporating new knowledge management technologies with existing legacy systems can present technical difficulties, demanding substantial time and resources to guarantee compatibility and smooth functioning. To tackle these obstacles, a thorough change management approach is necessary. This should encompass employee training, transparent communication regarding the advantages of the new KM tools, and a staged rollout to facilitate gradual adjustment.

Organizations should thoroughly assess the cost-benefit ratio of new knowledge management technologies and explore scalable options that can be adapted as the organization's requirements and resources evolve.

Moving forward, the area of knowledge management is set to advance quickly, propelled by various factors that are expected to transform the ways organizations handle and utilize knowledge. A key trend is the growing adoption of advanced analytics in the field of knowledge management.

As organizations produce and gather extensive data from numerous sources, big data technologies are making it possible to derive significant insights from this information on an unparalleled scale while keeping intact. Within the realm of knowledge management, big data analytics can be employed to uncover patterns, trends, and relationships in how knowledge is accessed, enabling organizations to gain a clearer insight into knowledge utilization and to identify areas where enhancements or advancements can be made (Abdalla, 2022; Furht & Villanustre, 2016).

Moreover, big data technologies can improve the capability to customize knowledge distribution, guaranteeing that employees obtain the most pertinent information tailored to their individual roles, preferences, and previous actions.

This trend is expected to promote a transition toward more data-centric knowledge management methods, where the management and distribution of knowledge are progressively guided by quantitative analysis and predictive modeling.

Artificial intelligence and machine learning are poised to significantly change the landscape of knowledge management in the future. These technologies can automate numerous labor-intensive activities linked to knowledge management, including the organization of information, recognizing pertinent knowledge resources, and suggesting content to users (Ferraris et al., 2019; Khan & Vorley, 2017).

AI-powered systems can enhance knowledge discovery by examining extensive datasets to reveal concealed connections and insights that might otherwise remain overlooked. For instance, chatbots and virtual assistants driven by AI can offer employees immediate access to information by responding to questions and directing them to the relevant resources, thereby enhancing both efficiency and user satisfaction. In addition, machine learning algorithms have the capability to enhance the precision and pertinence of knowledge suggestions over time by adapting based on user interactions and feedback.

With the advancement and increased accessibility of artificial intelligence and machine learning technologies, they are anticipated to play crucial roles in KM systems, allowing organizations to handle knowledge more efficiently and accurately.

An additional developing trend in knowledge management is the increasing significance of knowledge management within this context. In a remote or hybrid work setting, conventional face-to-face methods for sharing knowledge are frequently impractical, which makes digital knowledge management tools and platforms vital for sustaining the flow of organizational knowledge. This transition has emphasized the necessity for knowledge management systems that are accessible from any location, facilitate asynchronous teamwork, and are easy for employees operating from various sites to use.

As remote work establishes itself as a lasting element in numerous organizations, knowledge management strategies must evolve to address the distinct challenges and advantages presented by a distributed workforce (Duan et al., 2019; Intezari & Gressel, 2017).

This involves making sure that information is readily available to employees working remotely, promoting a sense of community and teamwork even when distances are involved, and tackling any security issues that may arise from accessing sensitive information from off-site locations.

The growing dependence on remote work is expected to foster additional advancements in knowledge management tools and methodologies, emphasizing improvements in connectivity, collaboration, and access to knowledge within virtual settings.

5.2 Emerging Systems Empowered by AI for Knowledge Management

The manner in which an organization generates, disseminates, and reutilizes its existing knowledge influences the degree of sustainable competitive advantage and expansion in the digital economy. This process, in turn, is fueled by the strategic application of knowledge (Latinovic & Chatterjee, 2019; Yilmaz, 2016).

As stated by Argote and Fahrenkopf (2016), knowledge serves as the fundamental element in enhancing organizational performance. When all conditions align with the organization's needs, it becomes an essential asset for gaining a competitive advantage.

Consequently, the approach of businesses is to continually create new ideas that promote innovation throughout all levels of operation and influence employee interactions, thereby improving performance.

Organizations can utilize strategic tools to analyze intricate tangible elements, such as tacit knowledge, in order to effectively manage physical resources. Nevertheless, there are obstacles in distributing resources toward knowledge activities due to the challenge of measuring the extent to which the results of knowledge interactions correspond to the measurable units of physical resources (Wang et al., 2016). Moreover, the realization that the economy is transitioning from conventional markets to a progressive knowledge-driven market is compelling proof to adopt knowledge as a viable method for maintaining market presence and competitive advantage (Eilert et al., 2017). The advancement of organizational procedures and performance in the last 10 years has been significantly facilitated by state-of-the-art technologies, including data analytics, artificial intelligence (AI), and business intelligence tools.

The developing capabilities of artificial intelligence (AI) are expected to influence almost every aspect of organizational structure and operations, including knowledge management (Olan et al., 2022).

Recent studies indicate that AI plays a crucial role in enhancing services and boosting the overall economy during this digital age (Huang & Rust, 2018; Olan, Liu, et al., 2021; Olan, Suklan, et al., 2021).

The increase in performance is now more reliant on creative products and services, functioning not just as a cooperation among various departments, units, and teams but also as a movement toward maintaining uncertain elements and disseminating expertise to promote growth, keeping as it is.

Furthermore, studies indicate that organizations are adapting to AI by transforming their competitive business processes and innovative strategies (Parkes & Wellman, 2015). Implementing a robust AI strategy that utilizes various techniques (such as machine learning and expert systems) across multiple business areas—including production, operations and supply chain management, human resources, strategic management, finance, and marketing—can enhance the collaborative decision-making process between AI and humans in each of these functions.

It can facilitate the advancement of AI-augmented business operations across various areas, such as capacity planning, scheduling, inventory management,

Table 5.1 Artificial intelligence strategy applied in different AI-enhanced business functions and areas of application

AI-powered business function and area of application	AI-enhanced practices	Source/citation
Human resources management and organizational behavior	– Automated recruitment using classification-based techniques – Turnover prediction – Candidate search and data acquisition from résumés – Performance management and career planning – Workforce planning – AI-based emerging jobs (e.g., machine relations manager) – Shifting from management of human resources (HR) to management of human-AI resources (HAIR)	Shukla (2009), Strohmeier and Piazza (2015), Buzko et al. (2016), Agrawal et al. (2017), Wilson et al. (2017), Huang and Rust (2018), Ojanperä et al. (2018), Plastino and Purdy (2018), Upadhyay and Khandelwal (2018), Brown et al. (2019), Li et al. (2019), Kreutzer and Sirrenberg (2020)
Production, operations, and supply chain management	– Forecasting using machine learning techniques – AI-based scheduling – Supply chain management using expert systems and machine learning techniques – AI-supported production planning and control – Inventory management – Capacity planning – Facility layout – Product and process design – AI-enhanced robots in manufacturing	Metaxiotis et al. (2002), Chaudhry and Luo (2005), Crone et al. (2006), Ławrynowicz (2007, 2008), Benyoucef and Jain (2009), Min (2010), Tsadikovich et al. (2010), Yu (2011), Hadavandi et al. (2012), Gunasekaran and Ngai (2014), Pérez-Romero et al. (2015), Abbasi and El Hanandeh (2016), Morabito (2016), Kumar (2017), Zor et al. (2017), Burggräf et al. (2018), Baryannis et al. (2019), Hagemann et al. (2019), Kreutzer and Sirrenberg (2020)
Strategic management	– Strategic decision-making with expert systems – All levels of organizational decision-making (tactical, operational, and strategic) using machine learning – AI-human collaborative strategic planning and strategy formulation – Digital business strategy	Knoppe (2000), Rosso (2004), Li and Li (2009), Morabito (2016), Jarrahi (2018), Kuncoro et al. (2018), Duan et al. (2019), Nieto et al. (2019)

(continued)

Table 5.1 (continued)

AI-powered business function and area of application	AI-enhanced practices	Source/citation
Marketing, sales, and customer service	– Social media analysis – Market knowledge generated from big data in B2B marketing – Automated market-basket analysis for cross-selling and upselling marketing using association rule – Recommendation/recommender system within e-commerce – Forecasting customers' buying behavior. – Predicting customer's lifetime value – Estimating the priorities/size of target markets	Cavique (2005), Zhang and Qian (2012), Martínez-López and Casillas (2013), Stalidis et al. (2015), Akerkar (2018), Syam and Sharma (2018), Paschen et al. (2019), Capatina et al. (2020), Kreutzer and Sirrenberg (2020)
Financial management	– Financial forecasting in the stock market – Credit risk assessment/evaluation using classification-based techniques – Prediction of bankruptcy for banks/companies via machine learning – Financial security and detection of fraud	Butler (2009), Ghodselahi and Amirmadhi (2011), Fletcher (2012), Abdou et al. (2017), Corea (2019), Kreutzer and Sirrenberg (2020)

Source: Younis and Adel (2020)

recruitment, workforce planning, performance management, and marketing research, along with the prediction of demand, consumer purchasing patterns, and financial outcomes (Table 5.1).

Artificial intelligence (AI) encompasses a range of information communication technologies (ICTs) that imitate human intelligence functions, primarily aimed at enhancing tasks, increasing efficiency, and fostering economic development (Arakpogun et al., 2021). Conversely, knowledge is the essential element that allows AI advancements to enhance the worth of intelligent agents and systems (Robbins, 2019). Intelligent agents (IA) developed through AI efforts possess a wealth of expertise essential for enhancing productivity and generating new insights for business operations.

An AI-driven strategy involves leveraging artificial intelligence to make important information available to employees through technology-based platforms. Moreover, AI possesses a diverse set of abilities that enhance an organization's innovation strategies through deliberate knowledge activities. This revival is fueled by proof that competitive advantages in various industries are more constrained and crucial for expansion (Olan et al., 2022).

AI offers a support for decision-makers within the organization to encourage knowledge-sharing activities that will be advantageous for both the workforce and the organization itself (Argote, 2013, 2015). When confronted with a new challenge, determining the specific type of knowledge needed by IA can be difficult. Consequently, creating essential knowledge maps is crucial for the successful implementation of AI-KS, making it a top priority. The growing adoption of advanced technologies has enhanced effectiveness, efficiency, and productivity, as both existing and new knowledge within an organization continually advance AI capabilities.

As a result, AI is capable of spotting redundancies in business operations and recommending the best use of resources to enhance performance. Nevertheless, the absence of a cohesive integration between existing and newly acquired knowledge complicates the determination of the specific type of knowledge necessary for AI to effectively enhance organizational performance. As a result, organizations consistently encounter ongoing difficulties related to their operational procedures, competition, technological progress, and the pursuit of innovative solutions in a rapidly evolving society.

Developments in IT are commonly regarded as driving forces behind organizational transformation initiatives in the context of knowledge management research (Tsui, 2005). Recent advancements in deep learning have significantly enhanced the ability of algorithms to replicate human functions, including "visual perception" (image recognition), "auditory perception" (voice recognition, natural language processing), and "decision-making" (analytical processing). With a wealth of available data and enhanced computational capabilities, these AI tools are progressively being adopted for commercial purposes (Canhoto & Clear, 2020; Jarrahi et al., 2023; Kaplan & Haenlein, 2019).

These AI tools utilize a range of methods to imitate human cognitive abilities, such as supervised machine learning (ML), neural networks, and deep learning.

The most effective deep-learning algorithms usually utilize a supervised approach. In this method, large amounts of labeled data are employed to modify the connection strengths between nodes in a large, multilayered computational network. This method allows for the recognition of patterns within the training data, which can subsequently be utilized to generate accurate forecasts regarding future, unknown data (Brynjolfsson & Mitchell, 2017).

This method differs from conventional knowledge management systems, like expert systems, which utilized symbolic logic where humans articulated and supplied the rules to the system. Since AI and KM are inherently connected to the concepts of knowledge and learning, recent progress in AI can establish new bases for revolutionizing KM within organizations (Sanzogni et al., 2017).

Within this domain, there exist two complementary techno-organizational approaches: (1) knowledge management, which specifically addresses the administration of knowledge within organizations, and (2) AI, recognized as a subset of computing that concentrates on creating systems capable of imitating human knowledge and learning processes. Organizations should explore the possible functions of emerging AI technologies in enhancing their knowledge management processes, given the evident link between the two. While traditional rule-based knowledge management offers valuable lessons, the distinct nature of modern deep learning as a different computational approach necessitates new perspectives on the possible connection between AI and knowledge management (Jarrahi et al., 2023).

5.3 Technologies to Support the Knowledge Management

The KM software is experiencing significant growth as an increasing number of organizations recognize the benefits of utilizing KM practices to enhance their enterprise value. The tools employed to facilitate KM initiatives are changing swiftly, as new providers emerge while some others exit the market. Of special significance in the context of technology's influence on knowledge management (KM) is the function of AI in its different manifestations. Over the past 20 years, AI has gained significant focus and has been extensively utilized across various sectors in the business world (Liebowitz, 1997; Mentzer & Gandhi, 1993; Metaxiotis et al., 2003; Metaxiotis, Askounis, & Psarras, 2002; Metaxiotis & Samouilidis, 2000; Metaxiotis, Samouilidis, & Psarras, 2002; Tafti & Nikbakht, 1993; Zhang et al., 1998).

The primary categories examined in this analysis include expert systems (ES), artificial neural networks (ANN), and intelligent agents (IA).

Expert Systems (ES)

Expert system (ES) is a software application that possesses extensive knowledge within a specific area and applies advanced reasoning processes to carry out tasks typically performed by a human specialist, keeping as it is (Welbank, 1983).

An ES is a computational platform that encompasses a structured collection of information, designed to replicate the problem-solving abilities of an expert within a specific field of knowledge.

The system can attain a level of problem-solving proficiency akin to that of an experienced human when faced with complex issues in the field (BCS, Expert Systems Specialist Group) and accomplishes this at an expert level of performance.

According to Hendriks and Vriens (1999), the term *knowledge* is prevalent in both the fields of knowledge management and ES. To identify the primary drawbacks or constraints of utilizing ES technology in the knowledge management, it is possible concentrate on these key issues:

(a) Expert systems cannot address unusual or ambiguous inquiries, nor can they provide unclear responses.

(b) The maintenance and updating of the knowledge base present numerous challenges.
(c) Expert systems cannot independently learn from experience.

The core of an ES is its knowledge base, which holds the information required to address a particular issue. To systematically document knowledge online and create knowledge repositories within KM systems, these techniques for knowledge acquisition can be utilized.

The understanding of ES can be depicted through various techniques of representation. Various approaches exist, such as semantic networks, frames, and predicate logic; however, the technique that is most frequently employed is the "if-then" rule, which is also referred to as production rules. The KM domain can leverage these methods, along with the associated "lessons learned" (both successes and failures), to assist in the codification of knowledge within knowledge management systems.

Conversely, it has been suggested that traditional rule-based expert systems depend on the premises of certainty and rationality, which focus on determining the optimal solution among distinctly available options (Fowler, 2000).

This differs from the field of knowledge management, which operates on the premise of uncertainty, subjective interpretations, and beliefs, as illustrated by the notion of *tacit knowledge*.

Artificial Neural Networks (ANNs)

Artificial neural network (ANN) is a method used for information processing that is inspired by how biological nervous systems, such as the brain, manage data. The core idea behind ANNs lies in the configuration of the information processing framework. A neural network system consists of many highly interconnected processing units, referred to as *neurons*, which are linked together in networks. This system employs a human-like method of learning through examples to address issues (Fausset, 1994; Haykin, 1994).

Each neuron processes an input, activation, and output function on its net input—which is the total of weighted input signals—to determine its output. The neural network is tailored for a particular task, such as classifying data or recognizing patterns, through a process known as *training*.

Similar to biological systems, learning entails modifications to the synaptic links that connect the neurons. To put it differently, the information that has been *learned* is kept as numerical values known as *weights*, which are allocated to the links between the processing units within the network.

This method is regarded as entirely distinct from what is utilized in ES, as it lacks a defined knowledge base and consists solely of a collection of relationships between data derived from empirical evidence. Thus, it cannot be asserted that ANNs have expertise in a particular domain.

Their role is to deliver a "black-box" transformation of input data into outputs, relying on prior *learning experiences*. The primary benefit of this technology is its ability to function with incomplete information, allowing it to generalize and showcase clear intuition. Moreover, artificial neural networks seem to function more similarly to the brain, presenting significant possibilities within the knowledge management framework.

They are also adept at creating user profiles, allowing information to be tailored to specific individuals based on their interests and preferences. Knowledge management can utilize this technology to enhance the dissemination and sharing of knowledge. Rather than relying on a passive distribution method where individuals must initiate access to the organization's knowledge base, a dedicated module (*knowledge distributor*) could be responsible for assessing and disseminating knowledge to the relevant individuals and stakeholders. Conversely, a limitation of ANN technology is that ANNs require their inputs to be in numerical format to apply the learned weighting algorithms.

This differs from an ES, which also takes symbolic inputs (object-oriented analysis). Naturally, this stands in opposition to the field of knowledge management, which presupposes a reality grounded in entities and practical significance.

Intelligent Agents (IA)

An agent refers to a computer system that exists within a specific environment and has the ability to act independently within that environment to achieve its intended goals (Jennings & Wooldridge, 1998). Typically, agents possess a vast amount of knowledge, professional experiences, and beliefs that they draw upon to complete their responsibilities. Research on intelligent agents has emerged as a key area within distributed artificial intelligence (DAI) (Knapik & Johnson, 1997; Metaxiotis, Psarras, & Papastefanatos, 2002; Murch & Johnson, 1998; Wagner, 1998).

Intelligent agents vary from objects in several respects. Smart agents interact with objects to carry out their functions (you can consider an intelligent agent as an object equipped with a head!). The actions of intelligent agents (including both the tasks they carry out and the methods they use to complete those tasks) can be altered in real time, thanks to learning or the impact of other agents. Intelligent agents are able to function autonomously, can analyze their own behaviors, and have the capacity to move.

They can proactively and flexibly work together to address challenges, utilizing protocols related to tasks and domains (a key objective is to reach agreement on solutions even when knowledge or data is partial or inconsistent). Within this framework, smart agents can assist in the search and retrieval processes of knowledge within KM systems.

Moreover, they can be highly effective in aiding the integration of knowledge, which will ultimately result in the generation of new insights. By engaging in diverse knowledge interactions, intelligent agents are capable of generating various viewpoints on the same scenario. These viewpoints might help increase the range of potential solutions, thereby enhancing the quality of the decision-making process (Carneiro, 2001). In addition, intelligent agents can be utilized to assess knowledge and distribute relevant information and insights (e.g., summaries, suggestions, and results) to individuals who ought to utilize it.

Many organizations recognize the necessity of systematically and transparently managing knowledge-related activities to enhance their competitive standing. Unless management openly endorses and supports initiatives to collect, organize, convert, document, and disseminate knowledge, valuable human and intellectual resources will be squandered.

Knowledge management appears to offer decision-makers improved support quality aimed at facilitating real-time adaptive active decision-making assistance. Nevertheless, organizations continue to require information technology, including certain elements of AI, to enhance and disseminate knowledge.

5.4 Applications of AI Systems for Knowledge Management

According to Jarrahi et al. (2023), it is possible to analyze the potential applications of AI systems for knowledge management processes (*knowledge creation, knowledge storage and retrieval, knowledge sharing, knowledge application*) and then broach possible ways through which a synergistic partnership between humans and artificial agents in organizational knowledge management can be achieved (Table 5.2).

Knowledge Creation

The process of creating knowledge might sometimes entail formulating concepts and solutions from the ground up; however, it more often consists of reorganizing and merging preexisting knowledge (Bhatt, 2001; Davenport & Prusak, 1998). Moreover, organizations can gain insights from outside sources (Alavi & Denford, 2011). Consequently, the process of knowledge creation can manifest as the acquisition of knowledge by seeking out or obtaining information.

Deep-learning AI's knowledge-generating capabilities stem from its ability to predict outcomes, such as estimating sales probabilities. This is the ability to use existing information to generate new insights that you did not have before (Agrawal et al., 2017). Deep-learning AI can uncover previously unknown patterns in the organization's datasets because of its ability to generate rules based on analogous patterns found in the data.

For example, AI can generate fresh inquiries and create new bodies of declarative knowledge within fields by linking variables in innovative manners. This can only be achieved through the development of self-learning analytical abilities and capabilities for recognizing patterns, enabling organizations to leverage big data in ways never seen before (Faraj et al., 2018).

Table 5.2 Potential AI applications in different KM processes

The KM process	Possibilities created using AI systems	Examples of use cases
Knowledge creation	• Fostering predictive analytics via self-learning analytical capacities • Recognizing previously unknown patterns • Sifting through organizational data and discovering relationships • Developing new declarative knowledge	• Forecast sales probabilities • Discover organization inefficiencies by analyzing CRM records
Knowledge storing and retrieving	• Harvesting, classifying, organizing, storing, and retrieving explicit knowledge • Analyzing and filtering multiple channels of content and communication • Facilitating knowledge reuse by teams and individuals	• Organize and summarize legal precedents relevant to a new case • Retrieve dispersed nuggets of information related to a troubleshooting situation
Knowledge sharing	• Connecting people working on the same issues by fostering weak ties and know-who • Facilitating collaborative intelligence and shared organizational memory • Generating a comprehensive perspective on knowledge sources and bottlenecks • Creating more coordinated, connected systems across organizational silos	• Facilitate feedback and peer review on communication systems (e.g., slack) • Facilitate real-time smart sharing between marketing channels and sales pipelines
Knowledge application	• Enhancing situated knowledge application by searching and preparing knowledge sources • Offering more natural and intuitive system interfaces (e.g., voice-based assistants) • Promoting equitable access to knowledge without fear of reprisal or social cost	• Find and apply question-answer pairs in online manuals to manage service knowledge • Provide more human-centered and accessible applications of knowledge through chatbots

Source: Jarrahi et al. (2023)

Comparable methods can aid organizational knowledge management since numerous organizations gather and preserve significantly more knowledge than they are capable of utilizing. AI technologies can likewise assist organizations in uncovering unforeseen relationships and insights within data collections that encompass customer interactions, such as call transcripts, email communications, enterprise chat systems, social media discussions, and entries in customer relationship management (CRM) databases (Lavenda, 2019).

Knowledge Storage and Retrieval

One important role of knowledge management (KM) is to establish and sustain an organizational memory that monitors both the knowledge resources created and those obtained. Efficient methods for storing and retrieving information are key components for maintaining organizational memory (Alavi & Leidner, 2001). This procedure is primarily aimed at gathering knowledge, clarifying it, and systematically documenting it for future application, frequently through the establishment of knowledge repositories. The value of AI in knowledge management is particularly clear in improving the organization and access to explicit knowledge.

Given that deep-learning AI is fundamentally linked to big data (Brynjolfsson & McAfee, 2017), these data-centric, self-educating algorithms create new opportunities for the collection, classification, organization, storage, and retrieval of the vast amounts of data produced by organizations. This includes data that was once considered too complex and challenging to analyze (Paschen et al., 2020). For instance, artificial intelligence can locate, categorize, and condense earlier legal cases that are pertinent to a present case (Bhattacharya et al., 2019). Moreover, AI has the capability to evaluate various forms of content and communication, produce summaries, identify pertinent subjects related to emerging issues, extract proprietary and confidential information, and offer reusable insights that can be readily applied to new scenarios.

Knowledge Sharing

Sharing knowledge across the organization is essential for effectively utilizing it in problem-solving and decision-making. However, the exchange of knowledge is frequently hindered by barriers related to time, space, and, more noticeably, functionality. Consequently, in numerous organizations, the sharing of knowledge often occurs in a localized and scattered manner. AI can help dismantle these organizational barriers in two primary ways: (1) by uniting individuals tackling similar challenges despite being divided by various boundaries or locations and (2) by establishing more integrated coordination systems, which provide managers with a clearer understanding of knowledge limitations. A major obstacle in knowledge sharing is breaking down silos to link various individuals with the information and practices they require (Jarrahi, 2019).

AI methods can address this issue by identifying and enhancing weak connections, thereby promoting learning within communities. In this regard, the primary application of AI for sharing knowledge relates to its role in fostering collaborative intelligence, which cannot be achieved through conventional database systems. AI can stimulate innovative thinking, foster a collective memory among diverse team members, and aid in providing feedback and peer evaluations.

These intelligent functionalities are progressively integrated into corporate or personal communication platforms like Slack or Yammer, offering more than merely a communication conduit for linking employees. AI systems are also capable of creating dynamic social graphs that illustrate the relationships among individuals and teams, offering an in-depth view of knowledge sources and areas of obstruction within the organization (Jarrahi, 2019).

Knowledge Application

Knowledge application involves utilizing information in real-world situations after it has been accessed or communicated. It frequently entails restructuring existing knowledge resources (such as a collection of best practices) into practical solutions or providing new products and services in a different context (Bhatt, 2001). AI can enhance the application of knowledge by offering quicker and more efficient access to knowledge resources, in addition to systematizing and automating procedures that assist employees in utilizing and integrating specialized knowledge (Alavi & Leidner, 2001; Cranefield & Prusak, 2016). New AI-driven tools, such as smart assistants, enhance the capture and presentation of knowledge required for the practical use of contextual information (Maedche et al., 2019).

This tackles a significant challenge faced by knowledge repositories regarding the application of knowledge: "getting the right knowledge to front line workers in real-time" (Davenport, 2019). Traditional knowledge databases are often difficult to navigate when a prompt response is required. In contrast, smart assistants can facilitate the easy access of existing knowledge for processing through AI-driven storage and retrieval methods, such as automated content cleaning, classification, and tagging (Davenport, 2019; Ransbotham et al., 2020). The situational understanding provided by AI proves to be highly beneficial in customer service, where a knowledge worker requires quick access to prior cases and an overview of the present problem.

AI systems are capable of offering more engaging and user-friendly interfaces that can communicate with or discuss topics with the knowledge worker in common language. As an illustration, natural language processing is a form of artificial intelligence that allows machines, such as digital assistants or chatbots, to comprehend and mimic human dialogue. These more organic and human-like methods of engaging with retrieval systems can aid in the application of knowledge. Chatbots are capable of offering information and assistance in its usage by engaging in natural dialogue with individuals. This can lower social obstacles that hinder equitable access to organizational information. A striking illustration can be found in how chatbots are utilized in higher education to assist students in accessing institutional knowledge and enhancing their sense of support from the university (Agrawal et al., 2017). The chatbot enables students to inquire in a relaxed manner, similar to chatting with a friend via text, and get suitable responses.

5.5 Future Trends in Knowledge Management

The adoption of new technologies consequently creates greater expectations for organizational employees regarding their skill sets. The emergence of new technologies necessitates that organizational employee gain updated knowledge and skills to maintain and enhance their competence in carrying out tasks and activities (Nyikes, 2018). Moreover, it is important to highlight the significant impact of contemporary technologies like virtual and augmented reality in training employees and enhancing their understanding, specifically in sharing the knowledge accumulated within the organization (Buntak et al., 2020).

In discussing the spread of knowledge, it is important to highlight both cloud computing and its application within the organization for sharing information and insights. Cloud computing offers access to the accumulated knowledge, meaning that the data compiled can be utilized by any authorized employees who are permitted to access and leverage the organizational knowledge gathered.

Industry 4.0 provides numerous advantages to organizations by enhancing the efficiency and effectiveness of their processes. However, it also introduces several challenges, particularly regarding the security of data stored in databases. Cyberattacks on organizations are becoming more complex, and the likelihood of emerging attacks is increasing. Consequently, cyberattacks can lead to the theft of sensitive information and trade secrets, potentially jeopardizing an organization's survival or disrupting its business operations (Pereira et al., 2017). This highlights the need to recognize and assess risks, along with establishing the strategies that will be used to eliminate those risks.

Cyberattacks may lead to the theft of valuable organizational knowledge, potentially threatening the competitive edge of organizations. Information security is especially critical for any organization that keeps data about its clients, including customers, as well as data gathered from various processes that the organization intends to utilize for analysis and to develop organizational insights (Hutchins et al., 2015). Networking organizations encounter the specific challenge of safeguarding information, which implies that they might decide to withhold or share the knowledge they possess with stakeholders connected to the network.

Nevertheless, individuals with a stake in the network might exploit their authority and obtain access to the organization's information via cyberattacks or alternative methods. This poses a risk to the organization that needs to be eliminated (Marabelli & Newell, 2012).

Digital transformation refers to the adoption of advanced systems and automated solutions that leverage artificial intelligence expertise. In recent years, artificial intelligence has been recognized as a means to identify and convert implicit organizational knowledge into well-defined knowledge. The problem of artificial intelligence in organizations pertains not solely to its application within expert systems but also to its role in automated processes.

Consequently, artificial intelligence presently lacks the ability to understand the context of specific tasks assigned to it that might potentially harm the organizational environment (Sanzogni et al., 2017). The issue at hand is whether artificial intelligence can genuinely supplant human intelligence and expertise. Additionally, there is a concern regarding the potential risks to individuals if AI starts to take over tasks that have traditionally been performed by people.

In real-world applications, artificial intelligence is starting to be utilized in the healthcare sector, where it functions within expert systems to aid medical staff in their decision-making processes (Furmankiewicz et al., 2014).

Additionally, there is presently no adequately developed artificial intelligence system capable of interacting with humans. Nonetheless, present knowledge management systems have incorporated certain types of artificial intelligence, enabling a range of capabilities, including knowledge extraction (Tsui et al., 2000). Integrating artificial intelligence into organizational knowledge management systems is crucial due to the roles these systems play and the complex activities they often need to perform (Birzniece, 2011). Birzniece (2011) suggests that connecting the knowledge base to artificial intelligence facilitates the programming of such systems and the establishment of algorithms that can execute tasks with minimal involvement from organizational staff. In other words, revising operating instructions simplifies the process of establishing automated system settings that enhance present operations. The importance of implementing such systems will be highlighted in relation to advancing cognitive computing, which encompasses various functionalities, including automated learning systems, motion detection, speech recognition, and more.

By incorporating technological advancements such as sensors within organizations, a substantial quantity of data is gathered and stored in the database. To utilize the gathered data for decision-making purposes, an analysis is required (Ruzgas et al., 2016).

Using mining techniques, it is feasible to retrieve and recognize organizational knowledge from the database. In this context, techniques for knowledge identification are categorized into data classification. This process involves organizing data into separate groups that allow for the identification of knowledge. It begins with the creation of data clusters, followed by the classification of data within the same group.

Ultimately, conditional formatting is applied to determine if any connections or correlations exist between the individual data points (Silwattananusarn & Tuamsuk, 2012). Additionally, there are various methods to extract knowledge from big data, largely determined by the nature of the data involved (Fayyad et al., 1996). Techniques in big data and data mining can be valuable for utilizing identified information for purposes like quality enhancement, production scheduling, and process optimization, among others (Cheng et al., 2018). Data mining should not be viewed merely as a means of extracting knowledge from vast datasets; it should also involve uncovering the existing knowledge that is often concealed within organizations. This hidden knowledge often arises from poorly articulated communication among employees and a lack of commitment from management to properly document and gather this information.

The digital transformation of organizations is essential due to the changes and innovations stemming from the advancements of industry 4.0. In addition to that, as the organizational environment grows more complex, organizations must adjust to the changing circumstances. By adapting to the updated demands, organizations gain fresh insights that allow them to create a competitive edge in the marketplace or distinguish themselves from their rivals.

There is a lack of research addressing the digital aspect of knowledge management within organizations. Additionally, the knowledge gained by the organization needs to be effectively managed. Present organizational knowledge management frameworks need to evolve to meet new circumstances. Organizations must establish novel frameworks to collect organizational knowledge, considering that digital transformation allows them to utilize new technologies for sharing knowledge throughout all levels of the organization, as well as implementing automated systems frequently powered by artificial intelligence.

Moreover, due to the escalating threats posed by cyberattacks, it is essential to incorporate a risk identification and risk management framework within the knowledge management model. This method can enhance the security of the knowledge produced.

Industry 4.0 offers various benefits and opportunities for organizations, focusing on enhancing the efficiency and effectiveness of their processes while also enabling the generation of organizational knowledge using artificial intelligence. Conversely, numerous obstacles arise when it comes to safeguarding knowledge that has already been developed. The process of digitizing organizational knowledge and saving it in databases carries the potential risk of cyberattacks, which could jeopardize both the security of the organization's information and the privacy of customers and users. The organization needs to adopt practices that guarantee the protection of all customer data to keep clients and all stakeholders' content.

The advancement and progress of an organization rely on its accumulated knowledge, which must be adjusted to meet new circumstances.

It is important to recognize that the knowledge profile of employees within an organization evolves, as the tasks performed often become automated.

Organizations are urged to establish a knowledge base and share the knowledge produced in alignment with the varied needs at different levels within the organization. This approach aims to form a strong competitive edge and enhance overall organizational performance.

References

Abdalla, H. B. (2022). A brief survey on big data: Technologies, terminologies and data-intensive applications. *Journal of Big Data, 9*, 107. https://doi.org/10.1186/s40537-022-00659-3

Agrawal, A., Gans, J., & Goldfarb, A. (2017). What to expect from artificial intelligence. *MIT Sloan Management Review, 58*(3), 23–27.

Alavi, M., & Denford, J. (2011). Knowledge management: Process, practice, and web 2.0. In M. Easterby-Smith & M. A. Lyles (Eds.), *Handbook of organizational learning and knowledge management* (pp. 105–124). Wiley.

Alavi, M., & Leidner, D. (2001). Knowledge management and knowledge management systems: Conceptual foundations and research issues. *MIS Quarterly, 25*(1), 107–136.

Arakpogun, E. O., Elsahn, Z., Olan, F., & Elsahn, F. (2021). Artificial intelligence in Africa: Challenges and opportunities. In *The fourth industrial revolution: Implementation of artificial intelligence for growing business success* (pp. 375–388).

Argote, L. (2013). *Organizational learning: Creating, retaining and transferring knowledge* (2nd ed.). Springer.

Argote, L. (2015). An opportunity for mutual learning between organizational learning and global strategy researchers: Transactive memory systems. *Global Strategy Journal, 5*(2), 198–203.

Argote, L., & Fahrenkopf, E. (2016). Knowledge transfer in organizations: The roles of members, tasks, tools, and networks. *Organizational Behavior and Human Decision Processes, 136*, 146–159. https://doi.org/10.1016/j.obhdp.2016.08.003

Bhatt, G. D. (2001). Knowledge management in organizations: Examining the interaction between technologies, techniques, and people. *Journal of Knowledge Management, 5*(1), 68–75.

Bhattacharya, P., Hiware, K., Rajgaria, S., Pochhi, N., Ghosh, K., & Ghosh, S. (2019). A comparative study of summarization algorithms applied to legal case judgments. In *Advances in information retrieval* (pp. 413–428). ECIR.

Birzniece, I. (2011). Artificial intelligence in knowledge management: Overview and trends. *Scientific Journal of Riga Technical University. Computer Sciences*, 5–11.

Biswas, T. R., Hossain, M. Z., & Comite, P. U. (2024). Role of management information systems in enhancing decision-making in large-scale organizations. *Pacific Journal of Business Innovation and Strategy, 1*(1), 5–18. https://doi.org/10.70818/pjbis.2024.v01i01.03

Brynjolfsson, E., & McAfee, A. (2017, July 18). The business of artificial intelligence. *Harvard Business Review*. Available at: https://hbr.org/2017/07/the-business-of-artificial-intelligence

Brynjolfsson, E., & Mitchell, T. (2017). What can machine learning do? Workforce implications. *Science, 358*(6370), 1530–1534.

Buntak, K., Kovačić, M., & Martinčević, I. (2020). Impact of digital transformation on knowledge management in organization. *Advances in Business-Related Scientific Research Journal, 11*(1), 36.

Canhoto, A. I., & Clear, F. (2020). Artificial intelligence and machine learning as business tools: A framework for diagnosing value destruction potential. *Business Horizons, 63*(2), 183–193.

Carneiro, A. (2001). The role of intelligent resources in knowledge management. *Journal of Knowledge Management, 5*(4), 358–367.

Cheng, Y., Chen, K., Sun, H., Zhang, Y., & Tao, F. (2018). Data and knowledge mining with big data towards smart production. *Journal of Industrial Information Integration, 9*, 1–13.

Cranefield, J., & Prusak, L. (2016). Managing your own knowledge: A personal perspective. In D. J. Pauleen & G. E. Gorman (Eds.), *Personal knowledge management* (pp. 121–136). Routledge.

Davenport, T. (2019, October 10). Managing support knowledge with AI: Talla helps Toast. *Forbes*. Available at: https://www.forbes.com/sites/tomdavenport/2019/10/10/managing-support-knowledge-with-ai-talla-helps-toast/#4d88ade77267

Davenport, T., & Prusak, L. (1998). *Working knowledge: Managing what your organization knows*. Harvard Business School Press.

Duan, Y., Edwards, J. S., & Dwivedi, Y. K. (2019). Artificial intelligence for decision making in the era of Big Data—Evolution, challenges and research agenda. *International Journal of Information Management, 48*, 63–71. ISSN 0268-4012. https://doi.org/10.1016/j.ijinfomgt.2019.01.021

Eilert, M., Walker, K., & Dogan, J. (2017). Can ivory towers be green? The impact of organization size on organizational social performance. *Journal of Business Ethics, 140*(3), 537–549. https://doi.org/10.1007/s10551-015-2667-4

Faraj, S., Pachidi, S., & Sayegh, K. (2018). Working and organizing in the age of the learning algorithm. *Information and Organization, 28*(1), 62–70.

Fayyad, U., Piatetsky-Shapiro, G., & Smyth, P. (1996). From data mining to knowledge discovery in databases. *AI Magazine, 17*, 37–54.

Ferraris, A., Mazzoleni, A., Devalle, A., & Couturier, J. (2019). Big data analytics capabilities and knowledge management: Impact on firm performance. *Management Decision, 57*(8), 1923–1936. https://doi.org/10.1108/MD-07-2018-0825

Fowler, A. (2000). The role of AI-based technology in support of the knowledge management value activity cycle. *Journal of Strategic Information Systems, 9*(2/3), 107–128.

Furht, B., & Villanustre, F. (2016). *Big data technologies and applications*. Springer.

Furmankiewicz, M., Sołtysik-Piorunkiewicz, A., & Ziuziański, P. (2014). Artificial intelligence systems for knowledge management in e-health: The study of intelligent software agents. In *Latest trends on systems: The proceedings of 18th international conference on systems* (pp. 551–556).

Haykin, S. (1994). *Neural networks: A comprehensive foundation*. Macmillan.

Hendriks, P., & Vriens, D. (1999). Knowledge based systems and knowledge management: Friends or foes. *Information and Management, 35*(2), 113–125.

Huang, M. H., & Rust, R. T. (2018). Artificial intelligence in service. *Journal of Service Research, 21*(2), 155–172. https://doi.org/10.1177/1094670517752459

Hutchins, M. J., Bhinge, R., Micali, M. K., Robinson, S. L., Sutherland, J. W., & Dornfeld, D. (2015). Framework for identifying cybersecurity risks in manufacturing. *Procedia Manufacturing, 1*, 47–63.

Intezari, A., & Gressel, S. (2017). Information and reformation in KM systems: Big data and strategic decision-making. *Journal of Knowledge Management, 21*(1), 71–91. https://doi.org/10.1108/JKM-07-2015-0293

Intezari, A., Taskin, N., & Pauleen, D. J. (2017). Looking beyond knowledge sharing: An integrative approach to knowledge management culture. *Journal of Knowledge Management, 21*(1), 492–515. https://doi.org/10.1108/JKM-06-2016-0216

Ismail Al-Alawi, A., Yousif Al-Marzooqi, N., & Fraidoon Mohammed, Y. (2007). Organizational culture and knowledge sharing: Critical success factors. *Journal of Knowledge Management, 11*(2), 22–42. https://doi.org/10.1108/13673270710738898

Jarrahi, M. H. (2019). In the age of the smart artificial intelligence: AI's dual capacities for automating and informating work. *Business Information Review, 36*(4), 178–187.

Jarrahi, M. H., Askay, D., Eshraghi, A., & Smith, P. (2023). Artificial intelligence and knowledge management: A partnership between human and AI. *Business Horizons, 66*(1), 87–99. https://doi.org/10.1016/j.bushor.2022.03.002

Jassawalla, A. R. M., & Sashittal, H. C. (2002). Cultures that support product-innovation processes. *Academy of Management, 16*, 42–54. https://doi.org/10.5465/ame.2002.8540307

Jennings, N. R., & Wooldridge, M. J. (Eds.). (1998). *Agent technology: Foundations, applications, and markets*. Springer.

Kaplan, A., & Haenlein, M. (2019). Siri, Siri, in my hand: Who's the fairest in the land? On the interpretations, illustrations, and implications of artificial intelligence. *Business Horizons, 62*(1), 15–25.

Khan, Z., & Vorley, T. (2017). Big data text analytics: An enabler of knowledge management. *Journal of Knowledge Management, 21*(1), 18–34. https://doi.org/10.1108/JKM-06-2015-0238

Khorashaadizadeh, S., Tabarsa, F., & Karimiain, R. (2024). Identifying obstacles to creating knowledge enterprises in Iran from the experts' point of view. *Journal of Knowledge-Research Studies, 3*(1), 41–66. https://doi.org/10.22034/jkrs.2024.59998.1056

Knapik, M., & Johnson, J. (1997). *Developing intelligent agents for distributed systems: Exploring architecture, technologies and applications*. McGraw-Hill.

Kyoon Yoo, D., Vonderembse, M. A., & Ragu-Nathan, T. S. (2011). Knowledge quality: Antecedents and consequence in project teams. *Journal of Knowledge Management, 15*(2), 329–343. https://doi.org/10.1108/13673271111119727

Latinovic, Z., & Chatterjee, S. C. (2019, September 24). How AI is helping companies break silos. *MIT Sloan Management Review*. Available at: https://sloanreview.mit.edu/article/how-ai-is-helping-companies-break-silos/

Lavenda, D. (2019, August 28). Machine learning should make tech work for us—Not the other way around. *TechTalks*. Available at: https://bdtechtalks.com/2019/08/28/machine-learning-data-management/

Liebowitz, J. (1997). Knowledge-based/expert systems technology in life support systems. *Kybernetes, 26*(5), 555–573.

Lim, K. K., Ahmed, P. K., & Zairi, M. (1999). Managing for quality through knowledge management. *Total Quality Management, 10*(4–5), 615–621. https://doi.org/10.1080/0954412997596

Maedche, A., Legner, C., Benlian, A., Berger, B., Gimpel, A. H., Hess, T., Hinz, O., Morana, S., & Sollner, M. (2019). AI-based digital assistants: Opportunities, threats, and research perspectives. *Business and Information Systems Engineering, 61*(4), 535–544.

Malhotra, Y. (2005). Integrating knowledge management technologies in organizational business processes: Getting real time enterprises to deliver real business performance. *Journal of Knowledge Management, 9*(1), 7–28. https://doi.org/10.1108/13673270510582938

Marabelli, M., & Newell, S. (2012). Knowledge risks in organizational networks: The practice perspective. *The Journal of Strategic Information Systems, 21*, 18–30.

Mentzer, J., & Gandhi, N. (1993). Expert system in industrial marketing. *Industrial Marketing Management, 22*(2), 109–116.

Metaxiotis, K., Askounis, D., & Psarras, J. (2002). Expert systems in production planning and scheduling: A state-of-the-art survey. *Journal of Intelligent Manufacturing, 13*(4), 253–260.

Metaxiotis, K., Ergazakis, K., Samouilidis, E., & Psarras, J. (2003). Decision support through knowledge management: The role of the artificial intelligence. *Information Management & Computer Security, 11*(5), 216–221.

Metaxiotis, K., Psarras, J., & Papastefanatos, S. (2002). Knowledge and information management in e-learning environments: The user agent architecture. *Information Management & Computer Security, 10*(4), 165–170.

Metaxiotis, K., & Samouilidis, J.-E. (2000). Expert systems in medicine: Academic illusion or real power? *Information Management & Computer Security, 8*(2), 75–79.

Metaxiotis, K., Samouilidis, E., & Psarras, J. (2002). Artificial intelligence in production scheduling: Two decades of research and promises, invited paper. In *International symposium for scheduling 2002, CUREAC, Lake Hamanako, 3–6 June*.

Murch, R., & Johnson, T. (1998). *Intelligent software agents*. Prentice-Hall.

Nyikes, Z. (2018). Digital competence and the safety awareness base on the assessments results of the Middle East-European generations. *Procedia Manufacturing, 22*, 916–922.

Olan, F., Arakpogun, E. O., Suklan, J., Nakpodia, F., Damij, N., & Jayawickrama, U. (2022). Artificial intelligence and knowledge sharing: Contributing factors to organizational performance. *Journal of Business Research, 145*, 605–615. https://doi.org/10.1016/j.jbusres.2022.03.008

Olan, F., Liu, S., Suklan, J., Jayawickrama, U., & Arakpogun, E. O. (2021). The role of artificial intelligence networks in sustainable supply chain finance for food and drink industry. *International Journal of Production Research, 60*, 1–16.

Olan, F., Suklan, J., Arakpogun, E. O., & Robson, A. (2021). Advancing consumer behavior: The role of artificial intelligence technologies and knowledge sharing. *IEEE Transactions on Engineering Management*, 1–13.

Parkes, D. C., & Wellman, M. P. (2015). Economic reasoning and artificial intelligence. *Science, 349*(6245), 267. https://doi.org/10.1126/science.aaa8403

Paschen, J., Wilson, M., & Ferreira, J. J. (2020). Collaborative intelligence: How human and AI create value along the B2B sales funnel. *Business Horizons, 63*(3), 403–414.

Pereira, T., Barreto, L., & Amaral, A. (2017). Network and information security challenges within industry 4.0 paradigm. *Procedia Manufacturing, 13*, 1253–1260.

Ransbotham, S., Khodabandeh, S., Kiron, D., Candelon, F., Chu, M., & LaFountain, B. (2020, October 20). Expanding AI's impact with organizational learning. *MIT Sloan Management Review*. Available at: https://sloanreview.mit.edu/projects/expanding-ais-impact-with-organizational-learning/

Robbins, S. A. (2019). AI and the path to envelopment: Knowledge as a first step towards the responsible regulation and use of AI-powered machines. *AI Society: The Journal of Human-Centered Systems and Machine Intelligence, 35*, 391.

Ruzgas, T., Jakubėlienė, K., & Buivytė, A. (2016). Big data mining and knowledge discovery. *Journal of Communications Technology, Electronics and Computer Science, 9*, 5–9.

Sanzogni, L., Guzman, G., & Busch, P. (2017). Artificial intelligence and knowledge management: Questioning the tacit dimension. *Prometheus, 35*(1), 37–56.

Schulte, W. D., & Sample, T. (2006). Efficiencies from knowledge management technologies in a military enterprise. *Journal of Knowledge Management, 10*(6), 39–49. https://doi.org/10.1108/13673270610709206

Silwattananusarn, T., & Tuamsuk, K. (2012). Data mining and its applications for knowledge management: A literature review from 2007 to 2012. *International Journal of Data Mining & Knowledge Management Process*, 13–24.

Spectre, L. (2019). Compartmentalized knowledge. *Philosophical Studies, 176*, 2785–2805. https://doi.org/10.1007/s11098-018-1151-2

Tafti, M., & Nikbakht, E. (1993). Neural networks and expert systems: New horizons in business finance applications. *Information Management & Computer Security, 1*(1), 22–28.

Tsui, E., Garner, B. J., & Staab, S. (2000). The role of artificial intelligence in knowledge management. *Knowledge Based Systems, 13*(5), 235–239.

Wagner, G. (1998). *Foundations of knowledge systems: With applications to databases and agents*. Kluwer Academic.

Wang, Z. N., Sharma, P. N., & Cao, J. W. (2016). From knowledge sharing to firm performance: A predictive model comparison. *Journal of Business Research, 69*(10), 4650–4658. https://doi.org/10.1016/j.jbusres.2016.03.055

Welbank, M. (1983). *A review of knowledge acquisition techniques (or expert systems)*. British Telecommunications Research Laboratories, Technical Report.

Yilmaz, R. (2016). Knowledge sharing behaviors in e-learning community: Exploring the role of academic self-efficacy and sense of community. *Computers in Human Behavior, 63*(2016), 373–382. https://doi.org/10.1016/j.chb.2016.05.055

Younis, R. A. A., & Adel, H. M. (2020). Artificial intelligence strategy, creativity-oriented HRM and knowledge-sharing quality: Empirical analysis of individual and organisational performance of AI-powered businesses. In *The annual international conference of the British Academy of Management (BAM) 2020: Innovating for a sustainable future, London, United Kingdom, 2–4 September*.

Zeynep, E., von Krogh, G., & Nonaka, I. (2008). The quality of group tacit knowledge. *The Journal of Strategic Information Systems, 17*(1), 4–18. https://doi.org/10.1016/j.jsis.2008.02.002

Zhang, G., Patuwo, B., & Hu, M. (1998). Forecasting with artificial neural networks: The state of the art. *International Journal of Forecasting, 14*(1), 35–62.

Conclusion

6

The book focuses on strategic role of knowledge management for the efficient governance of organizations. Knowledge management is the new capacity of dealing with intangible resources and creating value for society.

Knowledge management serves as a strategic asset that enhances organizations' abilities to gain a competitive edge. Effective managers have come to understand that the value of their organization increasingly hinges on its capacity to manage knowledge efficiently. A competitive marketplace demands a continuous effort in refining organization strategies and operations, along with adjusting to market fluctuations, all in pursuit of achieving sustainable long-term success and enhancing shareholder value.

The emphasis of management is transitioning toward the efficient handling of organizational resources, particularly in relation to knowledge and the associated processes of generating, documenting, sharing, and utilizing that knowledge.

As organizations recognize the significance of knowledge management as a key driver of their success, both practitioners and academics are starting to raise questions about the relationship between knowledge management and organizational performance. Numerous studies have found that the issue of organizational performance is more intricate than previously thought, extending beyond just conventional financial metrics. Research indicates that financial metrics alone do not provide a complete picture of organizational performance in today's economy; additional measures are necessary to gain a broader understanding of an organization's performance.

Practitioners and business managers alike agree that issues of technology, process, people, and content must be addressed to achieve success. Today, an organization must have *good enough* technology to make progress, especially in the transnational business environment. However, to achieve bottom-line success, even more attention must be paid to the other issues. The fundamental organizational element of knowledge management is the community of practice, consisting of

M. Valeri, *Organizations and Knowledge Management*, Knowledge Management and Organizational Learning 16, https://doi.org/10.1007/978-3-031-97954-5_6

individuals who have a shared area of expertise and/or who aim to find answers to shared challenges.

Cultivating essential communities is challenging even when members are situated in a single area with strong connectivity. When members are distributed globally, they share their knowledge in a cohesive manner throughout the organization.

Effective management of knowledge requires the use of AI. Concepts and technologies created by the AI community are essential for effective knowledge management. Various terms can be employed, such as corporate memory, knowledge repository, best-practices database, and others; however, an effective knowledge base is essential for successful knowledge management.

Insights gained in the AI community regarding knowledge acquisition, representation, and inference can be applied effectively to knowledge management. Members of the community should have the ability to locate and apply the pertinent information contained in the repository.

In contemporary knowledge management systems, the search engine serves as the primary powerhouse. Search engines utilize basic techniques for understanding natural language. We anticipate that, in the future, the knowledge gained regarding indexing and retrieval within case-based reasoning systems will be utilized. Additionally, the significance of agents and technology for distributed problem-solving will grow substantially.

The difficulties of knowledge management challenge AI. The problems mainly revolve around individuals, are widespread, and are quite complicated. Everyone plays a role in contributing. For effective implementation in knowledge management, AI technology needs to serve a wide range of individuals—specifically, the knowledge workers within organizations.

It is essential to keep in mind that they are not experts in computers. Understanding is not simply organized. Extracting it is challenging; it is transient and might only be roughly accurate. A major obstacle in developing expert systems is the challenge of acquiring knowledge, and this issue must be resolved to succeed in knowledge management as well. Nonetheless, there is a bit of positive news. The issue might be easier to address in the new setting. Systems designed for knowledge management generally do not aim to address an issue independently. Instead, they aim to gather insights (including best practices, lessons learned, advice, and solutions to similar issues, among others) that help individuals create their own answers.

In other words, the objective today is to assist individuals in finding solutions to their challenges. This does not imply that the AI community should abandon the objective of expert systems; instead, it highlights the knowledge management community's keen interest in providing substantial support to individuals as they tackle challenges.

In a knowledge-powered organization, the exchange and utilization of knowledge are commonplace. Consequently, the organization has significantly enhanced its performance while lowering its expenses.

Tools for data mining and knowledge discovery provide significant support. The emerging task for knowledge management will be to transform the organization into a supplier of products and services that can only be realized by effectively utilizing the combined expertise of its workforce.

While it is presently not feasible to envision the entire array of technological solutions needed to facilitate this new condition, those in positions of authority believe that AI technology will be crucial in this transition.

The manufacturer's authorised representative in the EU is Springer Nature Customer Service Centre GmbH, Europaplatz 3, 69115 Heidelberg, Germany. If you have any concerns regarding our products, please contact ProductSafety@springernature.com

Printed and bound by CPI Group (UK) Ltd, Croydon, CR0 4YY
30/09/2026
02225513-0007